seder stories

seder stories

passover thoughts on food, family & freedom

NANCY RIPS

CUMBERLAND HOUSE
NASHVILLE, TENNESSEE

SEDER STORIES

PUBLISHED BY CUMBERLAND HOUSE PUBLISHING INC.
431 Harding Industrial Drive
Nashville, Tennessee 37211

Cover design by Unlikely Urban Design, Nashville, Tennessee

ISBN-13 978-1-58182-643-2
ISBN-10 1-58182-643-5

Printed in the United States of America

2 3 4 5 6 7 8 9 10—12 11 10 09 08

To Steve,
who always said I could do it.

They tried to kill us.
We won.
Let's eat.

—*Anonymous*

P assover night is different from all other nights
because we remember the
most important moment in the history of our people.
On this night we celebrate our going
forth in triumph from slavery into freedom.

—*Leon Uris*

contents

introduction

Passover is the Festival of Freedom, and all Jews have their own memories. But who knew Seders took place in five-star restaurants, on Broadway, in a governor's mansion, in prisons, let alone that there is a zoo in Jerusalem that prepares diligently for the week of Passover?

Nobel Laureate Elie Wiesel said that Seders transformed his family. When the first prayer was said, he and his siblings were suddenly princes and princesses, and his parents became a king and queen. Pulitzer Prize–winning author Wendy Wasserstein recalls the day she made her stage debut—at a model Seder at the Yeshiva of Flatbush. And for actor Mandy Patinkin, Passover brings forth images of his Aunt Ida's one-of-a-kind red-glass Passover plates.

For me, Passover was all about never-ending food—briskets, chicken, matzah balls, and killer horseradish. And for my children, they remember Elijah, in person, strutting in the front door and playing a trumpet—loudly. Dressed head to toe in fashion-forward brown polyester, he annually made people drop to the floor.

Passover is America's most celebrated Jewish holiday. As Jews we enjoy it each year and love to tell stories about how we have observed it in the past.

seder stories

I

There's no seder like our seder

An introduction to the best-remembered, lovingly recalled Seders of long ago

In every generation, it is one's duty to regard himself as though he personally had gone out from Egypt.

—*The Haggadah*

Every year, right after Purim, my grandmother would paint her pantry. Eventually, the layers of white paint got so thick that the cupboard doors wouldn't close all the way. And the paint never quite dried. If you pressed your fingernail into it—months later, at Rosh Hashanah, say—you could still make a small curved impression. It was faint but you could see it. This never failed to fill me with wonder.

Into that magical pantry went the Passover dishes—clear and green and fragile. My grandmother let me help her stack them on the shelves.

I remember my mother and grandmother cleaning the house before Passover. They schlepped pots and pans down to the basement and schlepped other pots and pans up from the basement. They scoured every surface in the kitchen. They dumped chametz (leavened products) crumbs from drawers, shook them from pockets, and beat them out of rugs.

And all the time, they laughed. While polishing silver. While ironing curtains. To me, preparing for Passover looked like forced labor in a house of bondage. But to my mother and grandmother it was pure joy.

I also remember searching for chametz on the night before the Seder. In our shadowy, almost-dark house, my brother and I put small pieces of bread on the windowsills and then—by the light of a candle—we led our parents to the leaven. Solemnly, using a feather, Poppa swept the crumbs into a wooden spoon. Then Mother wrapped everything up in a cloth and put the whole bundle outside for the night.

In the morning, with much ceremony and many benedictions, we burned the chametz to ashes. Poppa told me that when the chametz went up in smoke, so did our evil inclinations. I didn't understand what he meant at the time. But I remember his words.

In my childhood, setting the Seder table was a serious business. Plates had to be strategically arranged on the lace cloth so as to cover up the indelible wine stains from past Seders. A chipped goblet? Give it to a family member and not a guest.

My special Seder responsibility was to make the salt water for the eggs, and the significance of the assignment was not lost on me. I measured and mixed and trembled. And when mother gave the water her taste-test, she always, always said it was perfect.

The Seders of my youth were combinations of order and bedlam. Poppa recited every single word. We wiggled and squirmed. When I carried my bowl and pitcher around the table so the men could wash their hands, I felt absolutely indispensable. And later, when everyone said, "This salt water is perfect," some tiny, undiscovered bit of chametz in me swelled with pride.

Who could really describe the food? The first taste of matzah. Poppa's five-alarm-grated-by-hand-with-some-of-his-knuckle-in-it chrain (horseradish). The knaidlach big as tennis balls. The potato kugel. The strawberry ices topping a cake that rose a foot tall from its silver platter.

I pitied the hungry, wandering Israelites who had to settle for manna from heaven. Then we sang the Hallel. My spoiled cousin Benji—as usual—found the afikomen (dessert matzo). A few new stains were on the lace cloth.

And finally, "Chad Gadya" and the verse about the Angel of Death. Oh, how those words terrified me. But curled up, half asleep in my grandmother's lap—wrapped tight in her arms—I sang bravely. And then the Seder was over.

So. That was then and this, as they say, is now. I'm a grownup, which means I now must create memories for my children and grandchildren. I do my best. But at Passover time, quite honestly, I'd much rather still be the kid.

—Ozzie Nogg

We were seder crashers. we didn't have the money for a passover seder when i was a kid, so our family would show up at relatives' homes unannounced.

—*Jerry Stiller*

When I was a child, the Seder consisted of the Kiddush and prayers about matzah, parsley, bitter herbs, the Four Questions, and dinner. Period. We used a Hagaddah provided by Maxwell House. I was never able to determine whether the Maxwells were Jewish, or if it was simply a marketing ploy by them.

—Al Abramson

* * *

My mother, Ann Landers, and I both felt a strong Jewish identity, but we had no Jewish information. So we spent Seders as guests of other families. I will not recount the Seder where, when Elijah was summoned to enter, a neighborhood cat sashayed in through the open front door. I will also pass over the Seders where some of the attendees were Justice Breyer, two Agnelli cousins, Prince Fredrik of Denmark, YoYo Ma, and even some Jews.

My most memorable Seder actually happened decades ago. My son, now thirty-nine, was then eight. He and his sisters, because of the circumstances of our lives, did not attend Sunday school, hence had no religious education. One year we went to a big Temple Seder for strays. It was held in a hotel ballroom. When the rabbi came to his traditional question, "What are the four kinds of people?" My son piped up, taking a breath: "A black, a white, a Japanese, a Chinese." The reaction from the assembled was an interesting combination of laughter and raised eyebrows.

—*Margo Howard*

* * *

Just imagine sixty people in your house for Seder! How would you feel if your responsibility was limited to covering only five pages of the Haggadah, serving just one course, and the best part—what if everyone left after twenty minutes?

In our neighborhood eight families did just that. They opened their homes for a progressive, traditional, slightly different, second Seder. Each was responsible for leading the group in a section of the Seder, along with serving a course of the meal. In addition, we asked every family to invite another to join the group. The ages ranged from preschoolers to grandparents.

We began at one home with a midrash about the necessity of observing the Passover holiday. Regardless of the level of knowledge, Halacha mandates that the observance take place. Having set the tone for the evening, we proceeded with Kiddush, the first cup of wine, and the dipping of the parsley. We then deviated from the norm slightly to serve appetizers of cut up carrots and celery, eggplant dip, and hard-boiled eggs.

Proceeding to the next home, we elevated the matzah, discussed its importance and broke the middle one, to be hidden as the afikomen. The five fifth-graders in the group were asked to sing the Four Questions.

On to the Ten Plagues part of the Seder. Our hostess, an art teacher, had decorated the area above their fireplace with colorful posters depicting the ten plagues in both

English and Hebrew, and their whole family presented a round-robin explanation of the story of the Exodus. We enjoyed matzah ball soup outside on the deck overlooking the pool.

Our main course took us to a different backyard deck. We devoured chicken wings, assembled on the grass for a group photo, and had a quick hunt for the afikomen.

We proceeded to the next house where we opened the door for Elijah and spoke of our hope for peace. We had the third cup of wine.

Up the hill we trudged (by now we were getting tired!) to the next-to-last home where we declared "next year in Jerusalem," sang Hallel, and were treated to fresh fruit salad.

Finally, on to our home where we served dessert and coffee and settled in for some post-Seder schmoozing. Some five hours after it had begun, the sun had set and our Seder had come to an end.

That night in April, sixty people observed tradition and created memories for ourselves and our children.

—Margie Gutnick

I always invited thirty-two people to each of our Seders. The first Seder was for family and the second for friends like George Burns, Sid Caesar, and Shecky Greene. I conducted serious Seders, and then we'd laugh till three or four in the morning.

—Jan Murray

* * *

As a Catholic, the only information I had about Passover was that the Last Supper had been called a Seder. In fact when they offered me something called gefilte fish, I thought it would be my last meal as well. I have learned in my short association with Jewish culture, that to be welcomed into a Jewish family means to be welcomed at their table. I've discovered that the story of Passover is the story of escape from persecution. After Treblinka and Dachau, I wonder how Jews can ever find the faith to pray for others.

It's a wonder I've learned to enjoy the Passover foods, even if I can't pronounce them!

—*Tim Rossi*

* * *

At my grandparent's house the table was extended as far as possible, then covered with a fresh white sheet, because who had a tablecloth that big? Every chair was called into service, including the piano bench which could cover two small tushes. Each member of the family was accounted for. There was no such thing as "I have to work and won't be there." It didn't even enter anybody's head—it was Yom Tov, the first Seder, and unless someone was hospitalized or dead, he was there.

—*Bert Lewis*

for many years, my husband, daughter, and I spent the first Seder at the home of Rabbi Gerson Cohen and his family. He was chancellor of the Jewish Theological Seminary in New York at that time, but our friendship stretched back much earlier. His mother had been my teacher at the little Jewish day school I attended as a child in Brooklyn. Later my husband and I both studied with him at the seminary.

Although we had become close to the Cohens, nothing prepared us for their Seders. We both had memories of large, noisy, family Seders, where the text of the Haggadah took second place to the fun of being with uncles, aunts, and cousins, and the refrain in the background was always the cry of "hurry up, we're starving."

There was no hurrying at the Cohens. Rabbi Cohen leisurely led us in reading every word of the Haggadah in Hebrew, stopping to explain a phrase, elaborate on a concept, or ask a provocative question. Soon we were all caught up in discussion, never noticing the passing hours. At some point, our little daughter would go into a bedroom to sleep, until she sensed that it was time to claim her afikomen present.

We often returned home well past midnight, and I would worry on the way about how we would get through the next night, the second Seder, which we held in our house for friends and family.

But here's what happened. Gradually, our second Seder took on the characteristics of the Cohens' first Seder. We had learned so much at that table, we wanted to share it with our guests, along with the excitement we had experienced of discussing, probing, and interpreting what we read. After Rabbi Cohen's death in 1991 and his family's move to Israel, we began conducting both Seders in our home. Each year now, as I prepare for the holiday, I search for new ideas to discuss and new insights to uncover in the ancient words of the Haggadah.

We make an effort not to conclude our Seders past midnight, but we don't rush them. The grandchildren usually fall asleep before the Seders end, but they manage to wake up in time for afikomen presents. And my daughter speaks with great affection of the Cohen years, forgetting her sleep times then and remembering only the love of learning that had enveloped that dear home.

—*Francine Klagsbrun*

* * *

My first and most lasting memory of a Passover Seder was as a child living in our shtetl in Czechoslovakia. I was anxiously "awaiting the call" to sing the Four Questions, and as the evening lingered on, I forced myself to stay awake with the adults. When it came time for welcoming the annual guest, Elijah the prophet, I approached the back door to let him in the house. Lo and behold, a beautiful white billy goat entered our home! To this day, I am still not convinced it was not his disguise.

—*Cantor Emil Berkvits*

When I grew up in the fifties, I loved our Seders. The men stayed around the table and the women would go back and forth and kibbutz in the kitchen and then join the men in the dining room. I remember my Bubbe, Mother, and her sisters always talking about what to make, who would make it, who would be coming to the Seders . . . just the planning of it was exciting.

—*Bette Kozlen*

* * *

Great Grandpa had nineteen children. Grandpa had fourteen; therefore, I was blessed with forty cousins within seven years of my age. Passover dinners were a hoot, with forty kids excitedly guzzling "wine" like the grownups. Only *we* were really given prune juice!

—*Shari Lewis*

33

We try and make Passover a modern holiday. There are always people coming from other countries. Last year we were in Seattle with our son and his wife and her father, who was attending his first Seder. He told us about leaving Puerto Rico in 1950 and moving to the United States.

—*Bob Kully*

* * *

My very earliest Passover memory is a shadowy recollection of arriving very late to a house and somehow understanding that the person who invited us was important to Daddy, so we needed to be good, even though we were tired. But I don't remember if my parents actually said that. The car and road were dark, but the house was bright. We were the only children, and everyone made a fuss over us. As we were leaving, we were given chocolate lollipops that were special, just for Passover. They came in a box with a plastic insert that had indentations shaped just like the lollipops. Then we went back into the dark and left the bright house.

On the other side of the family, my maternal grandfather was always trying to make Judaism come alive for us. He would tell us that when God created the world it was tovu vavohu, which means disorder or chaos. Then he would let us throw our toys all around the room. For Passover, in the middle of the Seder, he would escort us into our room, and we would take out all of our toys and toss them all around! Then they could all leave Egypt together to freedom!

—Aviva Segall

* * *

Our Seders have moved to the second generation. My husband, Milton, and his best friend led them together for years. Now they let one of the next generation conduct it.

One year recently our daughter-in-law planned a very child-oriented Seder, not like the one she remembers where everyone had to be quiet while the grandfather just "recited." The Seders are now held at her house, because only she can hold twenty-six people. She cooks the main things, like the matzah balls and briskets, but the adult children of both families bring the rest of the food.

—*Judith Viorst*

* * *

I have long described myself as a "lox and bagel and matzah" Jew. I grew up in a Jewish neighborhood in Philadelphia. We were culturally Jewish. While I did not attend synagogue services, on the High Holidays I would not have considered going to school; however, the family did get together for Rosh Hashanah dinner, but prayers were not a part of the procedure. Nor did we observe Shabbat.

Each year at Pesach everything changed! We always had a Seder, even if abbreviated. For a full week, not a morsel of bread, cake, grain, rice, lentils, or anything else unfitting passed into our mouths. I loved all the special cakes and cookies my mom prepared, and I so enjoyed fried matzah and matzah meal latkes! This was my favorite week of the year!

—*Diane Axel Baum*

* * *

I didn't grow up very religious. In Columbia, Maryland, you didn't have a choice of Reform, Conservative, or Orthodox. However, Passover was always a big event at our house. My father would make his own Haggadahs with quotes, poems, and thoughts pertaining to modern times, and we always invited Jewish and non-Jewish guests to our home. "Remember you too were strangers in Egypt" was something that was instilled into my upbringing. To this day, I live my life including "the stranger."

—*Jordana Glazer*

Our Seders included not only family members, but individuals who were alone and needed a place to be. Our dining room was a full house, both nights! My brother, sister, and I noticed that among our many visitors we had some very good reading voices. People took their parts seriously when it was their turn to read. It made us think that we should recognize the best of the bunch. And so the awards, the "PAWs" (Pesach Award Winners) began.

In the 50s, every store, especially Woolworth's and the corner drugstore, had rubbery funny-ugly-faced figures with long hair of varying colors that were called trolls. And from that came the inspiration for the Seder awards, the PAWs. The trolls cost ten cents a piece, and we bought a dollar's worth that first year. We spent a quarter on a bigger troll so that we could give a well-deserved award to our Mom. She deserved it for all of the wonderful delights that danced on our taste buds and made us happy and proud to be Jewish.

Award Ceremony Number One, 1958, was a hit! Our Uncle, with his beautiful baritone voice, not only read like a star but could sing like one as well! Our Father was the winner for interpretation. We handed out eleven awards in all, and while not everyone received a trophy, the following year, after the afikomen search, the awards ceremony was eagerly anticipated. We didn't disappoint! Each year was better and bigger, with varying categories and new winners!

—*Marcy Cotton*

* * *

Every year my in-laws do the same thing. My father-in-law hides the afikomen in the exact same spot, and the kids always pretend to be searching. When the service is over and it's time to find the afikomen, everyone acts surprised to discover the hiding place.

—*Ann Goldstein*

I grew up in Miami, and we would celebrate Passover with my father's cousins, Sydney and Rose, at their beautiful Miami Beach home. Sydney was a colorful character with a handlebar mustache and snazzy wardrobe. His wife was lovely but a bit ditzy. Her cook/housekeeper made the whole dinner and liberally used cooking wine in all the recipes. Everyone, even the kids, was served the regulatory four glasses of wine. One Passover, when my younger brother was about five, he spent the last half of the Seder under the table, barking like a dog—thanks to the four glasses of wine.

—*Carol Katzman*

* * *

As a child, every Passover Seder was at my mother and father's house. Then, while in her mid-50s, my mother died, and a year or so later it seemed my responsibility to host a Seder for the whole family, not a small group.

So we did. But we had nothing . . . only single copies of the Haggadah, no Seder plate, and absolutely no knowledge of how to prepare a Seder. And for me, even more of a problem, no notion of how to run the actual Seder.

The family was invited. The food was planned. Then I sat alone one evening with a Haggadah, starting to work on the service. To make things simple, I decided to use place cards for everyone, and I drew a simple diagram in a black loose-leaf notebook, along with small notes in my copy of the Haggadah with the names of who would read each separate part.

All went well. Everyone did their own part. And it seemed to me that I had been leading a Seder for years.

Then the next year came. There were place cards, plans, and a chart in the black notebook showing where everyone was seated so I could keep things moving along smoothly.

All of that was forty years ago. In each of those years, leading the Seder became much easier, I drew a little chart, sometimes before the Seder and sometimes after it was over, showing where each person sat around the table. After a while, the seating chart became important by itself, for year by year some family left town, some passed away, and some were born.

Today I read back to 1969 and find names of uncles and aunts now long gone. The little black Passover book has became a history of family. The little black Passover book, unlike other little black books, gets better to me as each year passes.

—*Dick Fellman*

* * *

A number of years ago, I attended Passover Seder at the home of Jack Carter, the comedian. Many of the guests were comedians, as well. Jack and his wife, Roxanne, were living in the San Fernando Valley, a location that has been a comic target for years, especially to those who resided in the nearby, much more upmarket zip code of 90210, who rarely ventured beyond the hills of Beverly.

When the Carter's son, Michael, asked of his father the very first "Why is this night different from all other nights?" Milton Berle brought the house down by saying, "Because we're in the Valley!"

—*Larry Gelbart*

* * *

I have a little gap. I grew up in Russia, and all Passover memories ended for me at age twelve when my father died. Now in America, we have begun many happy traditions and have been to wonderful Seders at different friends' homes.

—*Anna Mosenkis*

* * *

Passover, for me, was the majesty of the Seder table. The crisp white damask tablecloth, the gleaming sterling flatware, and the Rosenthal china my parents brought from

Europe. Passover was hiding the afikomen. It was opening the door for Elijah and racing back to the table to see whether the prophet was really visiting our home.

Passover was the nutty, wine-flavored charoset my brother and I could never get enough of and the grated white horseradish maror that made our eyes tear. It was the airy bubelach my mother would prepare for breakfast—fried golden mounds of stiff egg whites, egg yolks, and matzah meal, sprinkled liberally with sugar.

Many Passovers have passed. I am the mother now and the grandmother, lovingly preparing the house and the special foods. My mother passed away over thirty years ago, but she is with me when I use her frying pan to make paper-thin omelets that I will roll and slice into egg noodles, when I chop eggs in her wood cutting bowl, when I set out the gold-and-black trimmed dishes my father bought in the Orient and that my mother gave me when I married.

Passover is about missing my mother and my father and my father-in-law, who are no longer with us to lead the sedorim. It is about making room at the table for sons-in-law and daughters-in law and their traditions. It is about the bottle of dishwashing liquid my son Eli set on the damask cloth one year to bring comic relief to a tense moment. "Let's have a little Joy," he said, and we did.

Passover is about listening to our grandchildren recite the "Ma Nishtanah" and pretending that we don't know where they've hidden the afikomen. It is about watching my son-in-law as he fervently sings "Next year in Jerusalem" and leads the dancing around the living room sofa with my husband and sons and our seven-year-old grandson, who is enraptured and wide awake though it is past one in the morning.

Passover is about hearing my grandson say, "I want to go to Nana's house," and having him call me and exclaiming, "Right, I'm coming to your house for Pesach, Nana?"

"Absolutely," I told him.

—*Rochelle Kriche*

Growing up, my Mother was gay and my family was not religious. Our big family get-together was Thanksgiving, not Passover. We always attended other people's Seders.

When I was in middle school, in the late 70s, my mother was taking a college class in women's studies. That year we were invited to a feminist Seder.

In this Seder, God became a woman. We discussed matriarchs and omitted the patriarchs. We discussed that freedom from slavery meant freedom from a male-dominated society and male oppression. Even as a thirteen-year-old, I knew this was just TOO out of the box. My sister and I cringed to see where we would be invited for the following Seder.

Now as adults, my sister and I live far apart, but we each like to host our own Seders, because that way there are no surprises.

—*Patty Epstein*

I grew up with my grandparents, and Passover was always special. The kids would sit at a kiddie table that was actually a small card table attached to the big grownup table. Now that I have a child, when we have guests over and set up a smaller table attached to a bigger table, I get goose bumps and fear that my wife will make me sit at the kiddie table.

—*Hazzan Michael Horwitz*

* * *

Kushner family tradition proclaimed that each person was to have their own silver wine cup with their name engraved on it at their place at the table. The silver wine cups sat on aluminum coasters that caught the ten drops of wine tapped out for the ten plagues and were filled from a miniature bottle of Mogan David wine or grape juice, depending upon the drinker's age. These wine bottles were painstakingly washed each year to preserve the classic Mogan David label.

—*Marcia Kushner*

Passover was a big deal for our family. In the 20s when I was growing up, the Matzah Man would come 'round to our house about a month before Pesach. He'd sit down at the kitchen table with Mother and take her order. How many boxes of matzah did she need? How much matzah meal for the matzah ball soup and the baked goods? Then a couple of weeks later, he'd bring it around.

Finally, a day or so before Passover began, Mother would put me and my sister into our old Studebaker touring car and we'd head to an older part of town. There was a woman who kept a cow in her backyard, so we'd take along a big bucket to get milk. I don't know what it was about that cow that made it Kosher for Pesach!

—*Jerry Gross*

A question has been raised:
"In Judaism, what is more important—
the sabbath or Yom Kippur?"
All I know is that for me,
nothing compares with pesach,
with the cast of family and story
that transcends time and space.

—*Rabbi Earl A. Grollman*

When I was a little girl, we even washed the doorknobs when we got ready for Passover, and my mother made me go through every book and shake them out. God forbid someone would be reading a book and a crumb would fall out. I was fifteen years old before I saw the end of a Seder, because I was so dead tired by the time the first Seder came along.

—*Eleanor Bernstein*

ב

why is this seder different from all other seders?

A potpourri of Seders with a twist—
Broadway Seders, Seders for two hundred,
Seders in a governor's mansion, prison
Seders, and a zoo getting ready for Passover

To know what you prefer, instead of humbly saying "amen" to what the world tells you you ought to prefer, is to have kept your soul alive.

—*Robert Louis Stevenson*

The thing I liked best about my Passover is a custom I instituted when I worked in the theater as a young actor. I started the Seder at midnight so that my working friends who could not attend their own family celebrations were able to observe the festival. In some ways, this reenacted the story in the Haggadah in which the rabbi retells exodus so far into the night that his disciples had to come and remind him that it was time for morning prayers.

The only one of my friends who managed to miss the midnight Seder was Zero Mostel. A week later he yelled across Fifth Avenue, "THEO! I couldn't come to your Seder. I had matzah poisoning!"

—*Theodore Bikel*

Most newlywed couples can look forward to spending their first few Seders at the home of either the husband's or the wife's parents. (Some scholars wonder if the custom of having two Seders arose in order to satisfy both sets of in-laws.) But about a year after my wife and I were married, we invited two hundred people, many of them strangers, to our Seder, and we got the government to pay for it.

I was ordained a rabbi by the Jewish Theological Seminary in 1960 and entered the U.S. Army as a chaplain. My wife and I were married for only a few months when the army sent us to Fort Sill in Lawton, Oklahoma, where I was chaplain to a constantly shifting population of soldiers and some fifteen Jewish families in the town. I was expected to conduct services, counsel troubled men in uniform, supervise a Sunday school, and in the spring, run a kosher mess hall that would serve three meals a day for the eight days of Passover.

Many people had to cooperate to make that work. My wife planned the menus, came up with the recipes (how do you translate a recipe that serves eight so that it will serve two hundred?), and supervised mess-hall cooks who were utterly unfamiliar with such concepts as keeping meat and milk utensils separate.

The quartermaster's office was immensely helpful. Since they periodically had to order new dishes and silverware, they timed their order so they could give us brand-new utensils for the holiday and afterward put them into regular service.

Both Seder meals were attended by some two hundred GIs, some from traditional homes for whom missing a Seder would have been a serious deprivation and some only nominally Jewish who were surprised to discover how important it was for them to share a holiday meal with fellow Jews. This being the first Seder I had ever conducted, I struggled to maintain a suitable ratio between Hebrew and English and between reciting and eating.

The morning after the Seder, our kosher-for-Passover mess hall was open for three meals a day, meeting the needs of Jewish troops and the occasional non-Jewish buddy who heard how much better the food was at the Jewish mess hall.

When Passover was over, we inventoried the dishes and silver, thanked the cooks, counted up how many meals we had served, and looked back with profound satisfaction at how well everything had worked out.

I would go on to be a rabbi for another thirty years, but I would never again do anything as logistically complicated, or in many ways, as rewarding as those first Passover holidays.

—*Rabbi Harold Kushner*

* * *

Last year I observed Passover in a prison. I had been invited by Jewish "brothers" in the Horizon Interfaith dorm at one of Ohio's incarceration facilities. Jewish inmates attended along with the warden, a Muslim inmate, the prison chaplain and his wife, two corrections officers, an outside program volunteer, the director of the Horizon program, and a selected inmate from each of the six Christian families in the dorm.

The men prepared the Seder meticulously, and this was a difficult matter in a prison environment. Keeping kosher requires that all the regular dishes, utensils, etc. cannot be used during the eight days of Passover. But the men came up with creative solutions. For example, they encased the water pitchers in new plastic bags so neither water nor hands touched the nonkosher pitcher. The table, beautifully set with paper and plastic, held all the correct food, and at each place was a Haggadah in Hebrew and English.

Everyone participated. The youngest inmate asked the Four Questions. An empty chair waited for Elijah, and the door to the room was allowed to stay open. Only when Elijah was no longer expected, did the chaplain lock the door once again.

The leader asked to say a few words to the warden. "Thank you for giving us this opportunity to observe Passover like this, in a 'family.'" The room fell silent while he struggled with tears. "You have given us back something that cannot be replaced." The room fell silent. "You have given us something we haven't had in a very long time."

In that moment, the entire room experienced what Martin Buber called "authentic interfaith dialogue," a meeting in the sphere of between, where we moved beyond ourselves to a greater wholeness.

—*Madeline Trichel*

* * *

Cruises gear up for Passover every year with rabbis, matzah, and Seder menus. Our South Pacific holiday cruise aboard the *Pacific Princess* had gone without a hitch. The clergy ministered to their flocks, conducting services and presiding over special meals.

But something wasn't kosher about Passover. Everyone knew the eight-day holiday ended on Saturday. However, when the passengers arrived in the theater for Friday evening's Shabbat services, participants noticed a large halla.

Whispers bounced around. Should someone tell the rabbi or simply whisk it away? The ship's galley obviously had prepared its usual Friday-night halla, not realizing that Passover was still in effect, thus making the bread forbidden fruit.

Finally, someone recognized that all was right in the watery world, although Friday night would still have been Pesach normally; because the ship had crossed the International Date Line, there were two Thursdays that week, thus making eight Passover days after all.

Passover services were conducted in the ship's theater. They drew about forty people from the United States, Australia, and England, but a passenger from Beverly Hills discovered the chef didn't know how to make matzah balls, so she went into the galley and demonstrated the proper technique.

Whatever the itinerary, reasons for a Passover cruise abound. Observant Jews can avoid the Herculean home preparations that precede Passover. And it's a chance for several generations to share the holiday together.

—Molly Staub

My family consisted of my mom, dad, younger sister (all deaf), and myself. The terminology in those days was "hard of hearing." Today it is more politically correct to use "hearing impaired."

Passover was a fun time for all, most particularly for us. I pretty much controlled the conversation from the vantage point that I played interpreter and storyteller to my deaf audience.

We all know attention wanders. To alleviate this, using sign language unfamiliar to anyone else, we talked about everyone at the table right in front of them! When questioned by the extended family if I was passing the correct information about the Seder on to them, I replied, "Why, of course!" I'm sure they didn't understand why we would laugh uncontrollably at things. I think that, over the years, both sides got wiser, and I lost part of my job, but we still had fun!

—*Carole Greenberg*

Many people think they have a rough job getting ready for Passover—cleaning the cupboards, the stove, the oven, and beating the rugs. Before you feel too sorry for yourselves, consider getting an entire zoo up to par and "Kosher for Pesach"!

The work begins the week before Passover. All the silos that hold grain products for the animals have to be emptied and cleaned. All the sections start cleaning out the cupboards and kitchens in the various areas. The main zoo kitchen is cleaned of all bread products, and anything that is not specifically kosher is placed in a locked storage room and sold to a non-Jew. This room is sealed by our rabbi and not opened again until after the holiday.

Just like at home, floors and walls are scrubbed, refrigerators are cleaned, and every area gleams. All the public areas are cleaned from the snack shops to the bathrooms, and all the staff know that the zoo is a hametz-free zone for the duration. The employee coffee rooms are cleaned and the coffee cups replaced with plastic. New containers of coffee, tea, and sugar are purchased, and we are almost ready!

Since bread and bread products have not been brought into the zoo for the last few days, there isn't any left in the zoo. The rest of the animal food—such as fruit, vegetables, meats, and fish—arrive daily from companies that supply the supermarkets. So we don't have to worry about that.

You might wonder what we feed the animals used to getting bread with their meals. We substitute wherever possible, and just like all of us, they go without. Matzah crackers are purchased, which the primates love. The waterfowl are less happy, and the flamingos get positively glum. Rice is sometimes given to other birds, especially parrots, as matzahs can be lethal to them. Take this advice to heart: if you have pet birds at home, don't give them matzah crackers—it can kill them. Most of the animals can be fairly sensitive to a sudden influx of matzah into their digestive tracts, so give them more vegetables and keep an eye on them to make sure problems don't develop from that end.

One thing that keeps our staff busy during Passover is preventing the visitors from throwing food to the animals.

Their unwanted generosity can cause severe intestinal problems to our animals, even more than normal!

—*Beverly Burge*

* * *

Our group in California is called GLBT. That stands for gay, lesbian, bisexual, and transgender. We have our Seder at a temple in the desert, and we invite all the clergy in the area to participate. Our group works because it's neutral and doesn't represent any one branch of Judaism. This year we had a Hawaiian Passover theme with pineapple chicken, decorated chopped liver with hula dolls, and plastic leis for everyone. The guests were all asked to wear Hawaiian shirts.

—*Burt Fogelman*

Some five hundred psychiatric inpatients in Israel are known to be survivors of the Nazi Holocaust. Many of them have been hospitalized continuously for twenty to fifty years. Most of these patients received diagnoses of chronic schizophrenia, with no special attention given to the historical circumstances related to their psychiatric symptoms and disabilities.

In response to the need for a different approach to this population, a unique home for such Holocaust survivors was opened on February 1, 2000, adjacent to the grounds of the Beer Ya'acov Regional Mental Health Center in central Israel. The entire facility is planned for one hundred residents, who are housed in three buildings. Each building is a separate one-story structure with its own small kitchen and communal dining room. Each resident room has its own toilet and shower and houses two patients. Activities at the home include psychodrama, exercise, music therapy, and a weekly cinema club.

Directed by a professional social worker, the home is staffed twenty-four hours a day by nurses and nurses' aides trained in geriatric and psychiatric nursing. A social worker and an occupational therapist support this staff, and a psychiatrist and an internist on call from the regional center usually visit the home every weekday.

One turning point in defining this program as a home rather than an institution came on the occasion of the first major Jewish holiday in our setting, the Jewish festival of Passover, on April 19, 2000. Passover is celebrated with the Seder, a ceremonial dinner and collective recitation of the ancient Israelites' enslavement in Egypt and the subsequent Exodus. The Seder meal is traditionally a family experience, often charged with high emotions. Family members meet with other relatives whom they may not have seen for some time, and they often recall deceased relatives.

Many of the survivors in our home have no relatives, and they all have a personal history profoundly disturbed by inhumane and systematic physical and psychological torture. Although staff members were apprehensive about having a Seder, most of the patients participated in the communal singing and religious ceremonies and partook in the festive meal.

The case of Ms. A is an illustrative example. Born in 1927 in Hungary, Ms. A was raised by a foster family in Budapest. She was forced for economic reasons to leave school and begin working as a maid at the age of fourteen. Ms. A was seventeen when the Nazis began rounding up Jews in the Budapest ghetto in 1944, and she was able to survive as a prostitute. The rest of her story is not clear. It is known that she emigrated to Palestine and was a soldier in Israel's War of Independence. After the war she never married or adjusted to normal life.

Before she was released to the Holocaust Survivors' Home, she had been hospitalized for forty years in a crowded, privately owned institution. Usually introverted, she was diagnosed as having residual chronic schizophrenia. Ms. A blossomed at the Seder. She read the story of the Exodus, she sang, and she seemed to express emotions long dormant, remembering things "as they were."

—*Baruch N. Greenwald*

On the second Seder night I go to the Tonic Nightclub in New York, which is housed in the old Lower East Side Kedem kosher wine factory. The booths are made from the old wine kegs! Many New York musicians go to this Seder (by invitation only—but luckily I am a friend of the owner who, like me, grew up in the Lower East Side). Once, I shared the Four Questions with Sean Lennon. I was amazed he knew some Hebrew. I think Yoko once dated a Jewish man after John's death.

—Laurie Gwen Shapiro

* * *

Last year we carpeted and "draped" the garage to accommodate fifty-five people at one table. We even purchased a chandelier to hang in the middle. Everyone is welcome at our Seder.

—Deenie Meyerson

Sharing with Jews and non-Jews the historic account of man's inhumanity to man and the fight for freedom our ancestors endured makes Passover a very special time for me. As governor of the state of Hawaii, I have been honored to host Passover Seders for the past three years at Washington Place, the governor's mansion in Honolulu. Rabbi Itchel Krasenjasky leads the Seder for over a hundred guests.

My memories of past Seders with family established a strong foundation for me, which led to the official gubernatorial Seders. The children (or as we say in Hawaii, *keiki*) need to be involved to learn from us. Their laughter and joy during the Seders are a lasting memory. They are our future, and although we may think they are not involved at the moment, they are soaking up every word and tradition we repeat throughout the evening. They are the living legacy we leave behind. It is a story we must continue to tell year after year to remind everyone about the struggles we face and to keep hope, liberty, and freedom alive in our hearts and minds.

—Governor Linda Lingle

Until ten years ago, I did all the traditional stuff at Passover, but my husband Sam and I decided we needed a break from cleaning and cooking for the whole family. So this year we went to the Canyon Ranch in the Berkshire Mountains of western Massachusetts for the week of Passover. At Canyon Ranch, a rabbi presided over the Seder, and I lit the candles at our own table. The meal is the usual—matzah-ball soup, gefilte fish, and brisket (minus the high fat content). The rest of the holiday is spent hiking, working out, playing volleyball, and luxuriating in the Jacuzzi, on the massage table, or facial chair, plus the best part—we met new friends who liked doing Passover just the way we did. It was great. We came home totally relaxed. I'm never cooking for Seder again!

—*Phyllis Berman*

When our daughter Naomi was a freshman at Northwestern University, she could not come home, so we brought Passover to her. I cooked all of the food ahead of time, packed up the cooler, a small hot pot, the pots and pans, the Haggadot, and we drove eight hours to Chicago. There were no portable microwaves or toaster ovens, so I used the small hot pot like a double boiler to heat the food. We sat on the beds in the motel room and recited the Haggadah. We dined buffet style.

—*Evie and Stan Mitchell*

* * *

My favorite Seder was with Marlon Brando. You might remember him as Don Vito Corleone, Stanley Kowalski, or the eerie Col. Walter E. Kurtz in *Apocalypse Now*, but I remember Marlon Brando as a mensch and a personal friend of the Jewish people when they needed it most.

I got to know Marlon about thirty years ago through a mutual friend. His son, Christian, came to work for me in fisheries I owned in Alaska and Minnesota. Marlon impressed me as a dedicated parent. He would often call me to check up on his boy with all the tenacity and loving concern of a Jewish mother: Was he eating enough? Did he get to work on time? Was he hanging out with the right people?

Christian was a great kid. He worked hard, had a good attitude, and earned the respect of all his co-workers.

In the mid-1970s, when I would visit Los Angeles from my home in Minnesota, Marlon and I would get together. I was starting to become increasingly involved in my religion, and he would tell me with great pride and satisfaction about his support for Israel even before it became a state. Marlon explained that in 1946, two years before Israel achieved statehood, he desperately believed that the survivors of the Holocaust deserved to have their own land where they could live free from oppression and the anti-Semitic tyranny of the outside world.

True to form, Marlon put his money where his mouth was and donated all of his proceeds from the play *A Flag Is Born* to the Irgun, a Zionist political group dedicated to rescuing European Jewry and the establishment of Israel as an independent sovereign nation. He continued his donations and charitable work over the entire two-year run of the play as it went from Broadway to touring destinations around the United States.

"A people that have fought so hard to survive need and deserve their own land," he told me. "I did all that I could and actively supported Israel's statehood anyway I was able."

Marlon also told me with great emotion that his success in theater and movies was largely due to the Jewish people in New York who befriended and taught him. He warmly mentioned Stella Adler, the legendary acting coach who both taught Marlon his craft and housed him with her family while he was getting on his feet as an actor. He was also especially proud of the fact that he could converse in Yiddish, having learned it while living with her family.

One of my visits to Los Angeles coincided with Passover. I was not yet Orthodox and made plans to attend a Seder at a local synagogue with my sister. Marlon called me that very day and invited me out to dinner. I graciously declined, explaining that it was Passover and I was going to a Seder. Marlon became audibly excited over the phone and said, "Passover—I've always wanted to attend a Seder. Can I come with?" He had made me an offer I couldn't refuse. I told him it could be arranged and called the synagogue, adding one more to our list.

A short time later, Marlon called me back and asked if he could bring a friend. I said, yes, by all means, never thinking to ask his friend's name. I called the *shul* again. They were a little less patient this time and begrudgingly told me that they could squeeze one more person in, but this was absolutely the last one, as they were now officially sold out.

Still later that day, I received a phone call from a childhood friend of mine who had become a well-known singer/songwriter. Being Jewish himself, and hearing I was going to a Seder, he asked if he and his wife could go along.

The *shul* was unhappy to receive my most recent request, but somehow I softened the heart of the receptionist, and she agreed to let my people go—to the Seder.

I will never forget the sight of our table in the synagogue, Marlon Brando was to my left and sitting next to him was his guest. This was during the height of Marlon's involvement with Native American causes, and he had brought with him noted Indian activist Dennis Banks of Wounded Knee fame. Banks was dressed in full Indian regalia: buckskin tassels on his clothes and long braids hanging down from a headband, which sported a feather. My childhood friend Bob Dylan sat to my right, joined by his wife, my sister Sharon, and other friends.

At first the Seder progressed normally, without anyone in the temple noticing anything out of the ordinary. After about forty-five minutes, the rabbi figured out that ours was not your average Seder table. "Mr. Brando, would you please do us the honor of reading the next passage from the Haggadah," he said. Marlon said, "It would be my pleasure."

He smiled broadly, stood up, and delivered the passage from the Haggadah as if he were reading Shakespeare on Broadway. Mouths fell open and eyes focused on the speaker with an intensity any rabbi would covet. When he was done I think people actually paused, wondering if they should applaud.

Somewhat later the rabbi approached another member of our table.

"Mr. Dylan, would you do us the honor of singing us a song?" The rabbi pulled out an acoustic guitar. I thought he would politely decline. Much to my surprise Bob said yes and performed an impromptu rendition of "Blowin' in the Wind" to the stunned *shul* of about three hundred Seder guests. The incongruity of a Seder, with Marlon Brando reading the Haggadah followed by a Bob Dylan serenade, would have made for a good Fellini movie. Needless to say, everyone was both shocked and thrilled by this unusual Hollywood-style Passover miracle. The entire *shul* came by to shake both Marlon's and Bob's hands, and they actually paused and spent time with everyone.

Just a couple of years ago, Marlon called me up in Minnesota, out of the blue. We had kept in touch through the trials and tribulations he was going through with his family. "Louie Kemp," he said, "I've been thinking about you. Twenty years ago you took me to a Seder. I want you to know that I still think about it to this very day. In fact, I was thinking about it today and that's why I called you."

He continued to thank me and tell me of the special spiritual impact it had on him and how much he identified with a people freeing themselves from bondage and uniting to celebrate and remember that freedom.

He told me he was sending his three youngest children to a Jewish day school in Los Angeles. When I asked him why, he said, "Louie, don't you know that the Jewish schools are the best?" I could almost hear him smiling over the phone.

—*Louie Kemp*

A Times Square Seder takes place in three distinct spaces in New York, all on the same block of Forty-second Street. Along with sculpture and video art, the Seder features symbolic actions performed by political and religious leaders known for their concern with social justice. Last year former Manhattan borough president Ruth Messinger helped to officiate.

—*Melissa Shiff*

* * *

I give potluck Seders. One year we transformed our house into a Bedouin village. One Seder, plastic frogs were croaking at arriving guests. My friends say, "When you've sat through a lifetime of tedious Seders, go to Heidi's place and play."

It's like a giant party and teaching experience. The dress code is you have to be able to dance and eat excessively. It's snooze-proof.

—*Heidi Kahn*

Going to another family's seder is a bit like going to Europe on an exchange program: the people are doing the same things but in unfamiliar ways.

—*Unknown*

3

The four questionables

A serious chapter based on Shalom Aleichem's words: Even though Pesach comes once a year, Jews insist on asking questions all year long.

Like most Jewish children, I especially loved the Passover holiday. Solemn and joyous, it allowed us to escape time. Slaves of the Pharaohs, we followed Moses into the unknown, into the desert, up to Mount Sinai. His summons to freedom was stronger than fear.

The Seder transformed us. On that evening, my father enjoyed the sovereignty of a king. My mother, lovelier than ever, was queen. And we, the children, were princes. Even visitors—the travelers and beggars we had invited to share our meal—were messengers bearing secrets, princes in disguise.

How could I not love this holiday, which began well before the Seder itself. For weeks, we lived in a state of expectancy, of preparation.

The house had to be cleaned, the books removed to the courtyard for dusting. The rabbi's disciples assisted in making the matzah. Passover meant the end of winter, the triumph of spring.

Here I must interrupt my tale, for I see that I am using the past tense. Why? Because none of this is true anymore?

Not at all. The meaning of the festival and its rituals has scarcely changed. Only I have changed.

I still follow the rituals, of course. I recite the prayers, I chant the appropriate psalms, I tell the story of the Exodus, I answer the questions my son asks. But in the deepest part of myself, I know it is not the same. It is not as it used to be.

—*Elie Wiesel*

* * *

Abraham Joshua Heschel was fond of saying that the important thing in life is to ask the right questions. For this we need an occasion, a structure, a set of symbols to prod us, all of which are provided by the sensory delights of the Seder table.

—*Arnold Eisen*

Jews who long have drifted from the faith of their fathers are stirred in their innermost parts when the old familiar Passover sounds chance to fall upon them.

—*Heinrich Heine*

* * *

I feel that the greatest reward for doing is the opportunity to do more.

—*Jonas Salk*

* * *

My most distinct memory of Passover is my very Orthodox, very European grandmother always cutting off any attempt by my brother, cousins, and me to discuss the Haggadah. "Sit still and *daven*," she would command. We were perfectly willing to daven—recite the text by rote—but we also wanted to raise questions about the difficult parts of the text: how could God punish Pharaoh if it was God who hardened his heart? Was it fair to kill all the Egyptian first-born males? Why isn't Moses even mentioned in the Haggadah?

I think my grandmother was afraid that these questions would shake our faith. Her ploy didn't work. Now our family Seders are filled with questions and discussions. And yes they do shake faith, but faith without some occasional shaking becomes fundamentalism.

On the good side, my grandmother's gefilte fish has never been matched.

—Alan Dershowitz

* * *

We grew up in a Jewish atmosphere. Today kids have to be taught to be Jewish.

—Joe Kirshenbaum

On the eve of Passover, I chop apples and walnuts and cinnamon with wine, precisely as my parents and their parents chopped them. I mark the defeat of our enemies. In our kitchen, empires fall again.

—*Leon Wieseltier*

* * *

My dad was a doctor and spent several years in the China-Burma-India theater during World War II. When he returned home, my older brother greeted him. I was very young and I didn't recognize him. This really hurt him, and he vowed to get to know his children.

As time went on, he decided to take all of his family to Florida for Passover. He felt that we could enjoy the holiday, sun, and at the same time meet with our siblings and cousins. Each year we took a family picture, and one year, along with a copy of the annual picture, this letter arrived, dated "Passover 1976, Diplomat Hotel":

Dear Children,

In the years to come there will be many changes in the world, in our country, and most of all in us. In this picture, however, time will be at a standstill, and looking at this picture in the future, the wings of memory will take you back to these wonderful, glorious days of our family togetherness. May we have many, many more of these happy events.

With all our love,
Mom and Dad

—*Carol Feinhandler Gutstein*

For many Jews, Passover is the only time to think about what it means to be a Jew in the here and now.

—*Marge Piercy*

* * *

There are only two ways to live your life. One is as though nothing is a miracle. The other is as though everything is a miracle.

—*Albert Einstein*

* * *

Passover has always assumed a special importance in our family, as its message remains so relevant today and connects Jews to other people who remain in bondage of one type or another. At our Seders, I was taught to recognize that we Jews, who have borne such a heavy burden of suffering through the ages, especially during the Holocaust, have a special obligation to speak out against the oppression of fellow human beings, no matter what religion or ethnicity they might be. So I have always looked at Passover as a time to reflect on my own liberty, on those yet to cross their own Red Sea, and what we can do to help them taste freedom.

—*John Pollack*

* * *

ANCIENT PLAGUES:
Blood. Frogs. Vermin. Beasts. Pestilence.
Boils. Hail. Locusts. Darkness.
Slaying of the firstborn.

MODERN PLAGUES:
ALS. Parkinson's. Alzheimer's.
Juvenile diabetes. Arthritis.
Huntington's. Heart failure.
Paralysis. Cancer. Stroke.

Oppressed people cannot remain oppressed forever. Like the Exodus in Egypt, yearning for freedom eventually manifests itself.

—Martin Luther King Jr.

* * *

At our Seders, when it's time to fill Elijah's cup, we ask everyone to pour wine from their own glasses into the cup and express a personal wish for the future.

—Barbara Kaiman

* * *

I remember vividly the Seders of my childhood. First Seders were always at Bubbe and Zayde's. We were a big family: grandparents; four daughters, each of whom was married; four sons-in-law, who all worked in my grandfather's supermarket business; and nine grandchildren. Any pilgrimage to Bubbe and Zayde's was an important event, but on Pesach, it was unique.

Seder was a dress-up affair: suits, ties, the works. I used to think that this was odd. It made sense to dress up when you went to synagogue, but not to Bubbe and Zayde's. Seder was also filled with tremendous anticipation. My Zayde, may he rest in peace, was a legend in his own time, known by virtually everyone and generous to a fault. We knew that come afikomen time, he would come up with something spectacular.

Seder was usually called for 6:30, but we never got started until after 7:00; some family members always came late. Usually, one of the dads had to miss the first part of the Seder to watch the store. Finally, one of the parents would call down into the basement for all the kids to come up. By that time, all of our nice clothes were disheveled from furious games of kickball, "war," and other assorted opportunities to beat up on one another. We'd reluctantly trudge upstairs, only to be greeted by irate mothers, who would quickly try to tuck in shirts, comb hair, and make us presentable at the table.

Seating everyone was not easy. With just inches separating the backs of the chairs from the furniture on the perimeter of the living room, there was a lot of sucking-in of tummies to climb into those seats. Once the rest of us were settled, Zayde sat down in his big thronelike chair at the head of the table. We picked up our Haggadahs—Maxwell House, of course (what would you expect from a family in the grocery business!)—and began.

My Zayde was not what you would call a religious man, although in his own way, he was deeply sentimental and nostalgic. For him, the best part of the Seder was to see his grandchildren ask the Four Questions. One by one, as each of us became the younger old enough to ask, he would nearly burst with pride as we stood at attention and sang or read these few words. I can still see his ruddy face, tears welling in his eyes, as he pretended to follow along in the text but all the while soaked up our broken Hebrew singing or English reading.

I don't remember much more about the first part of our Seders. I do recall watching Zayde break the matzah for the afikomen, wrap it in a napkin, and stick it in his suit pocket, all with a sly smile toward the children. I'm sure he and some of the men said a few more parts, but I don't think it took more than thirty minutes before we were ready to eat.

I always knew it was time for the meal, because the men could take off their jackets and loosen their ties. The women headed for the kitchen to help Bubbe who—by the way—never sat down at the Seder. During the reading of the Haggadah, Zayde would call out to her, "Sit, sit," and she would call back, "I'm listening. I'm listening." If I hadn't learned later that this could be different, I would have thought it was part of the ritual that the hostess is not allowed to sit down until after the guests have left! Out came the fish and then the soup with huge, fluffy matzah balls, followed in quick succession by all the other dishes. While I learned later that the original Pesach meal in Egypt was eaten in haste, I suppose that we rushed through this huge dinner because it was late, and everyone was starved!

Seder nights are magic with their own memories and significance. We cannot return to the lessons of that first Seder night in Egypt without being enriched by the memories of our own Seder celebrations.

—*Ron Wolfson*

* * *

Memories are all we really own.

—*Elias Lieberman*

4

matzah for the masses

The Haggadah proclaims, "All who are hungry, let them come and eat."

Ye shall observe the feast of unleavened bread.

—*Exodus 12:17*

I do the Passover thing, with the lamb and all that stuff.

—*Roseanne Barr*

* * *

I remember my mother bringing home a giant, live carp fish and putting it in our bathtub to swim. She kept it there till it was time to make the gefilte fish. I used to squirm at the idea of this huge fish in our bathtub, and I wouldn't take a bath for days after that!

—*Hannah DeBruin*

* * *

Dining out for Passover is the new tradition. Every year at sundown on First Seder, some three hundred people gather at the Beverly Hills Spago for the ritual Passover dinner. Sitting at long community tables, Spago guests read the story of the Jews' exodus from Egypt, sing holiday songs, and dine family style at $250 per person. The prix fixe menu may seem expensive, but the restaurant donates a substantial portion of the money to Mazon.

The menu includes comfort foods customers are used to from grandma's house, but with a twist: white fish and salmon gefilte fish with Belgian endive and horseradish sauce, balsamic glazed Cornish hen stuffed with wild mushrooms and potatoes, assorted spring vegetables, and chocolate espresso truffle cake.

"The dispersion of families has created a market for dining out on Passover," explains Chef Allen Suser of Miami. "It used to be that Grandma would cook and Grandpa would sit at the head of the table and lead, but today's extended families are more distant."

—Beth Panetz

Every year the family went to Aunt Molly's for Passover. It was a very frightening experience, Aunt Molly cooked for three days, which sounds like a tough task, but it wasn't half as hard as having to eat everything she cooked. If you missed one matzah ball or spoonful of red cabbage, she attacked.

"What's the matter? You didn't like the horseradish?"

"It was great and I am going to put some on my brisket."

"So are you going to eat the brisket? You don't like my chicken?"

"If you eat the pancakes, then you won't have anything left for the red cabbage."

I only tell you this because it happened EVERY year and the dialogue was ALWAYS the same!

—*Art Buchwald*

My mother's mother would come to our house and help my mom with the making of the gefilte fish. What that involved was having me drive to the fishmonger to get buffalo, carp, and other fish that swam in the troughs on display. The wriggling fish would be selected, beheaded, and prepared in fillets. I was shocked by the methods used to reduce vibrant and active fish into strips in paper that seemed so warm and heavy when the packages were thrust into my hands. The cooking took place in huge pots of boiling water. The fish were placed in these caldrons, and the smell would rise along with the steam and noise of food preparation. Then came the grinding and the addition of a host of spices that made the smell even more pungent. I would watch in awe as these cooks did their work without recipes, without measuring devices, and with clear intent of completing a task of no small magnitude. Finally came the pillows of fish and the accompanying gel that my family's adult members relished and adored.

—David Herzog

One Passover my grandmother made a very large pot of soup. She put the matzah balls in a separate bowl to be passed around after the soup was ladled out. The bowl quickly got to my older sister Judy, and she began to eat the matzah balls. Some time later, a little voice was heard at the end of the table, "Do I HAVE to eat all the matzah balls?"

—*Jean Duitch*

* * *

Can we talk about what you're making for Seder?

—*Joan Rivers*

We decided to remember how sweet freedom is and planned to have an all-chocolate Seder. The invitations were Hershey wrappers glued to a note card that said—"Come and Celebrate the Sweet Taste of Freedom."

Each part of the Seder had something to do with chocolate, from the chocolate of affliction, the ten plagues of chocolate (thirst, cough, fat, diarrhea, worms, zits, etc.), and Hillel sandwiches made of s'mores. When it was time to taste a green vegetable, we brought out the green M&M's. Maror was a dark, bittersweet chocolate. The Four Questions began with, "On all other nights, we eat peanut butter, chocolate, or a combination of both. On this night, why only chocolate?"

The leader ended with, "We lift these three matzah and say: Praise be you, Creator of sweets and calories who has sanctified us by commanding our sweet tooth to eat of this delicacy."

—*Cheryl R. Skolnick*

My happiest memories were of all the women in my family spending two days together in my mother's large Passover kitchen in her tiny house. We each had our own responsibilities. I was my mother's sous chef. I chopped and cleaned the vegetables for the meats, soups, and gefilte fish. I ground the fish for my mother to season and prepare for the gefilte fish. My sister-in-law and my sister did the baking under my mother's direction, which they really did not need. My other sister-in-law cleaned and prepared the turkeys and made the Jell-O molds. My niece, who was the oldest grandchild, set the very long table for at least twenty-six. The sad day was when I put my Passover dishes away, because I loved everything about Passover.

—*Sylvia Wagner*

Our Seder in Natchez, Mississippi, carries on its own traditions, like matzah balls with gravy. Like any good southern Seder, the charoset is made with pecans, not walnuts. "Pecans just work better."

—*Jerry Krouse*

* * *

My grandfather, Zayde, didn't see too well, but he loved to clean and prepare the fish for Passover. We'd all go to the market, pick up the best-looking fish, bring it home, and put Zayde out on the back porch so he could get it boned, skinned, and ready for my mother. He'd put everything into his pot: the eyes, the tail, the bones, the fins. Then he would bring it to mom to finish.

May God not punish any of us, but to this day, I'm sorry to say, we never, never used his fish. Mom would buy already prepared gefilte fish, spice it up, and serve it. Everyone at our

Seders raved about Zayde's wonderful gefilte fish! He never knew. He felt he did his part, and that's what was important.

—*Marlene Kahn*

* * *

Why is this night different than all other nights? On all other nights I eat one dessert, but on this night I eat three. Then add on all the calories I consume throwing back the required four glasses of wine—and I'm becoming a real Thighmaster.

Passover, on the surface, seems like the single chick's ideal holiday. It's as if Atkins' trendy no-carb diet was actually inspired by our ancient ancestors who fled without bread. Pesach is the perfect week for a woman to watch her weight. It's an eight-day Exodus-endorsed break from carbohydrates. Yeah, right. And Eve was just looking to keep the doctor away.

Despite the divine ban on bread, I eat more carbs during Passover than during any other week of the year. If I ate matzah balls, but not matzah brie, Dayenu (enough). If I ate matzah pizza, but not matzah lasagna, dayenu. With string bikini season just weeks away, I'm scarfing just about any unleavened starch. I'm in my kitchen baking flourless chocolate cake, chametz-free banana cheesecake, and my mom's famous kosher-for-Passover strawberry whipped crème torte. It's just too much, but I love it!

—*Carin Davis*

* * *

My most vivid Passover food memories are of the Passover buns, or bulkies, or simply those dry tasteless buns. I remember taking sandwiches made with them to school every day and at the same time counting the days until this ordeal would come to an end. Would it be tuna fish or possibly salami today? Maybe even a chicken sandwich.

I remember the raised looks when we noticed a Jewish student entering the lunch line during Passover and wondering if he might be struck by lightning before he filled his tray with the forbidden food? Not to worry. No lightning, No disaster. But I really do miss eating those "bun" sandwiches!

—*Dr. Ben Nachman*

* * *

We would sit at the other end of the table from our uncle so we could sneak the carrots, pickles, and olives during the service. Now, during our "kid friendly" service, we actually serve appetizers as part of our service in the beginning.

—*Louri Sullivan*

* * *

My Bubbe made the Seders every year. She did it the old-fashioned way, before the days of food processors and microwaves. She probably wouldn't have used them anyway. She even thought canned goods were too modern.

—*Judy Rubin*

Even the poorest jew, a
recipient of charity, must, on
the eve of passover,
eat only in a reclining position,
as a mark of freedom,
and drink no less than
four cups of wine.

—*Mishnah: Pesahim 101*

I enjoy eating gefilte fish at Passover, even though my family isn't so keen on it!

—*Richard Dreyfus*

* * *

At first I joined Weight Watchers because I needed to lose weight. The group leader is Haya, who is so much fun to listen to, but she is not a thin woman. Israel is a bit more lax in this department.

Her pre-Passover speech to my group of women was like a coach's speech before the big game. "Go team, it's going to be rough, but you can do it."

In her opinion, Passover is the worst holiday for weight control. It's a lethal combination of festive meals, kids home from school on vacation, travel, and worst of all: matzah. It innocently looks like a low-calorie cracker, but don't let it fool you. One sheet of the crunch stuff is as fattening as two big slabs of bread. And that's before you fry it or load it up with butter or cream cheese or my family's favorite, chocolate spread.

But the toughest of all is the night of the Seder, when God practically commands us to stuff our faces. Haya's best tip for stopping yourself from eating like a pig: "Make sure you sit next to somebody really thin."

One woman in the group responded, "I don't think there's anyone in my family who qualifies."

—*Allison Kaplan Sommer*

* * *

friendships develop over food and wine.

—*Midrash: Biblical Text*

I never thought alcohol was a big deal. By the time I was two, I was already drinking Manischewitz with the family at Pesach. While this wine has all the personality of a concrete block, I grew to enjoy it a great deal, and it became sort of a holiday Kool-Aid for me. Our charoset was made with it, so I liked that especially.

I also dipped everything in wine, from the Hillel sandwich to the afikomen. It was pretty muddy by the time I was done with it. But I think Passover saved my adolescence just by virtue of the fact that I could drink with my family on Pesach and any other time I wanted, and so alcohol was just another thing to consume. Hooray for Manischewitz!!

—*Tamara Say*

A diet is when you watch what you eat and wish you could eat what you watch.

—*Hermione Gingold*

* * *

Man cannot live by unleavened bread alone.

—*Anonymous*

5

The Dysfunctional family seder survival guide

*A survival guide for the "good times" when
Aunt Rose, Uncle Joey, Cousin Phil, and
Niece Myra are all in the same room*

Say little and do much.

—*Rabbi Shammai, Talmud: Pirke Avot*

* * *

A family is a little civilization unto itself,
with its own history, laws, codes, and discontents.
—*Carol K. Howell*

Morris calls his son in New York and says, "Benny, I have something to tell you. However, I don't want to discuss it. I'm merely telling you because you're my oldest child, and I thought you should know. I've made up my mind. I'm divorcing Mama."

The son is shocked and asks his father what happened. "I don't want to talk about it. My mind is made up."

"But Dad, you can't just decide to divorce Mama just like that after fifty-four years together. What happened?"

"It's too painful to talk about. I only called because you're my son, and I thought you should know. You can call your sister and tell her. It will spare me the pain."

"But where's Mama? Can I talk to her?"

"No, I don't want you to say anything to her about it. I haven't told her yet. Believe me, it hasn't been easy. I've agonized over it for several days, and I've finally come to a decision. I have an appointment with the lawyer the day after tomorrow."

"Dad, don't do anything rash. I'm going to take the first flight down. Promise me you won't do anything till I get there."

"Well, all right, I promise. Next week is Passover. I'll hold off seeing the lawyer till after the Seder. Call your sister in New Jersey and break the news to her. I just can't bear to talk about it anymore."

A half hour later, Morris receives a call from his daughter who tells him that she and her brother were able to get tickets, and they and the children will be arriving in Florida the day after tomorrow. "Benny told me that you don't want to talk about it on the telephone, but promise me you won't do anything till we get there." Morris promises.

After hanging up from his daughter, Morris turns to his wife and says, "Well, it worked this time, but what are we going to do to get them to come down for Passover next year?"

—*Anonymous*

Pesach is a time for gathering together around the Seder table and reliving the liberation of our people from Egyptian bondage with signs and wonders.

Unfortunately, this ritual does not free us from enslavement to our extended family. The "signs" of that togetherness include elevated blood pressure, shattered nerves, and a churning in the pit of your stomach.

The following is a list of suggested strategies for dealing with the challenges and extracting some sense of kavannah (intention, direction) from the experience:

1. **Aunt Rose:** *Seeker of Attention and Child Spoiler Par Excellence.* Although well into her eighties, Aunt Rose continues to dress like Eva Peron. Childless herself, she gets her jollies out of spoiling all the children at the Seder and riling them up to the point where the children's table resembles a scene from *Lord of the Flies.* When her brother asks her to stop this, she replies, "Shut up! I'm still older than you are."

Strategy: Move her to the children's table and ask her to lead all the children in "Dayenu" and "Chad Gadya."

Assure her that your accountant knows Andrew Lloyd Webber personally, and that if she finds the afikomen, you'll prevail on him to write *Minerva: The Musical* with your aunt in the starring role.

2. **Uncle Joey:** *And His Latest Squeeze.* Twice divorced and in his sixties, Uncle Joey has arrived with his latest, a twenty-two-year-old fashion model from La Jolla who is into deep-sea diving, gangs, and Joey's investment portfolio. They arrive dressed in matching leather motorcycle outfits and enough medal chains to tie Hong Kong securely to the stem of the QE2. Throughout the Seder, the two of them keep dropping sprigs of parsley into each other's mouths, performing a veritable sonata of coos, giggles, and smooches.

Strategy: Suggest that their leather attire makes them the perfect candidates for acting out the passage "Slaves we were unto Pharaoh in Egypt" and volunteer them to do something original and kinky with the bitter herbs. If this fails, dress them up as a 1950s movie matron and shine flashlights at them.

3. **Cousin Phil:** *Thirty-five and Unmarried.* As punishment for having failed to produce a wife and the obligatory grandchildren, Phil's parents continue to relegate him to the children's table and make him recite the Four Questions. This precipitates an hour-long psychodrama worthy of the *Jerry Springer Show,* assuring that the kugel will be burned to a crisp, the charoset will start to ferment, and a curious brown layer of something will descend upon the gefilte fish.

Strategy: Hire an incredibly ravishing Israeli woman to play the role of Phil's date, resulting in an immediate elevation of your cousin's status and promotion to reciting "Avadim Hayinu" (We were slaves). If this fails, invite two members of the American Arbitration Association to sit between Phil and his parents.

4. **Niece Myra:** *The Collegiate Vegetarian.* A self-confessed vegan, Myra can only contain her militancy through the karpas (greens) ritual. The moment the company recites, "This is the bread of affliction," Myra begins her harangue about "how can you talk about affliction while you eat the flesh of exploited animals who spent their entire lives

in a feedlot, etc." And "You drink wine processed through labor of oppressed Mexican braceros, a wine filled with chemicals and preservatives, and you dare to talk about the ten plagues?" In spite of Grandma's attempts to make nice, Myra continues her diatribe that reaches its height when your father points to the shank bone.

Strategy: Present her with a Chia pet and suggest that she harvest its contents for next year's Seder. If this fails, invite her to spend next Passover back at her local food co-op's annual vegan Seder.

—*Rabbi Burt E. Schuman*

* * *

In the final analysis it is not what you do for your children, but what you have taught them to do for themselves that will make them successful human beings.

—*Ann Landers*

Every Seder featured at least one pain-in-the-neck relative who monopolized the conversation, and who asked the fifth question over and over, so often in fact, that everyone wanted to kill him/her. You don't remember the fifth question? It is: "When do we eat?"

Before you knew it, it was time to open the door for Elijah. You just knew that your dopey brother or some idiot cousin would be on the other side of the door dressed like a Bedouin in a feeble attempt to imitate some pathetic vision of Elijah. Yup, Elijah came to our Seder dressed in a bathrobe, wearing a towel turban-style on his head.

As the hour grew ever later, the Seder would quickly wind down. Before you knew it, it was all over. Another Seder the next day and then off to other pastures.

So here's the question: How come if all we ever do is complain about those Seders, we still have them every year?

—Rabbi Jeffrey Rappoport

Most of my childhood Passover memories have nothing to do with the Passover story itself. Like most American kids, I started out observing the Passover from a card table, fidgeting while the grownups read from the Haggadah.

I remember my cultivated Grandma Lil, dunking her finger into her cup and flicking wine out while reciting the ten plagues. She always tried to avoid the eyes of my Grandpa Herman, her ex-husband, because he had been one of her private plagues.

Later, I remember heated arguments about the Vietnam War, with my then hawkish young dentist father pitted against his brother, a UCLA sociology PhD student, and his sister, a Berkeley undergrad. My father's brother had a long hippie beard that shook like a burning bush when he shouted, "We're killing innocent people in 'Nam." My father's sister's breast shook and cords stood out on her neck when she yelled at my father, "You're sounding like one of the pigs." My father's father stepped in with his Yiddish-accented English and said, "Quiet, we're trying to have a

Seder here. What will the children think?" He motioned at me, age six, and my sister, age four. The Seder went on.

As I grew older, I was allowed into the grownup sanctum, the actual dining room. I felt almost adult as I helped carry steaming bowls of matzah ball soup, cleared the dishes, and conversed with my elders. At age fifteen, I heard my sweet widowed Grandma Bea sucking the marrow from a thick chicken bone. Suddenly the same tyrannical Herman screamed at her from across the table, "That's disgusting! You're not living in a shtetl anymore."

Grandma Bea ignored him and sucked louder. "I'm done now Sharon dear. You can take my plate." I scooped up her plate and tried to dash for the kitchen. Grandpa Herman grabbed my forearm, fixed his blue eyes on mine and said, "I hope you won't behave like her in polite society." I wanted to cry. But I followed my grandma's example, ignored him and walked out.

My Grandma Lil, tyrannical Grandpa Herman, and my father are all gone now, but those Seder memories remain. Growing up taught me that despite difficult relatives and challenging situations, the Seder must go on, the story must be told, the wine must be drunk, and the songs must be sung. Doesn't that somehow seem like a metaphor for the Jewish people?

—*Sharon Rosen*

* * *

I always looked forward to lively Seders. There was just an overabundance of food when I was a child. You had to have brisket in case someone didn't like chicken.

—*Jason Alexander*

* * *

My parents have always had dueling Seders. My dad calls his "My Zayde's Seder." It is a rapid-fire, singsong spew of Haggadah delivered, in his words, "with the same intonations, incantations, and misogynistic deprecations that have been handed down by rabbis to my grandfather thousands of years ago." In other words, he bangs on the table a lot and barks, "The women will be quiet!" This performance is only semi-intended as camp.

My mother's Seder, on the other hand, is all about cooperative learning and hands-on participation. As befitting a professor of education at the Jewish Theological Seminary, she finds neato lessons everywhere. In the past, we've compared and contrasted various kinds of Haggadot (feminist, archeological, Manischewitz, pacifist, Claymation). She's made game boards so we could play Jewpardy (with categories including Pharaoh Phacts and On the Seder Plate) and Jewish Family Feud. We've mimed the plagues, turned *The People's Court* into a one-act play in which Pharaoh was on trial (I was Rusty the bailiff), and slapped each other with leeks (don't ask). She incorporates multicultural readings, finds amusing Passover songs on the Internet, and invites questions and commentary from the group. My father assures readers of his Web site, "Believe me, God does not listen."

Last year Mom outdid herself. She had us tell the story of Passover through a combination of Haggadah reading and Paper Bag Players–style improvisation. She divided us into teams, gave each team a bunch of random props (dental floss, a plastic lei, a tape dispenser, a vintage Dukakis-Mondale button), and assigned each team a section of the Haggadah to act out.

Despite some kvetching, the family rose to the occasion. Some people went conceptual. My Aunt Belleruth's team used Arafat as a stand-in for Pharaoh; my brother used the pimping of baby formula in Third World countries as a metaphor for the killing of the firstborn. Some were more literal. My ninety-year-old grandmother played the youngest child reciting the Four Questions, with shoelaces—one of her team's props—tied in her short steel-gray hair like bows. She read the questions in a piping babyish voice while my cousin Abie stuck his arms under her armpits and made amusing hand gestures. My father rolled his eyes and muttered things that sounded suspiciously like *hillul hashem* (an abomination unto God).

Mom's Seder can be scary. You will be in a skit, and you will solo on "Echad Mi Yodaya" even if you do not know Hebrew. My mother resolutely refuses to see that this is terrifying. She hands people a transliterated Haggadah and sings encouragingly along with them. But hello! Still terrifying! Past guests have included Brown University students who tend to look like deer in the headlights when the solos start, as well as my mom's friend Mary, a nun (whose Hebrew is better than mine, so she's not a very good example), and my dad's Franciscan co-worker from a group home for troubled boys, Brother John. Everybody steps up to the mike; everybody represents Chad Gadya, yo!

When I said performance art, I wasn't kidding.

—*Marjorie Ingall*

* * *

If there's a will, there's a relative.

—*Anonymous*

M ost Jewish historians bury their heads in bagel dough in order to soften the images of their families. They tend to paint pictures of togetherness, happiness, bonding, peace, joy of family life.

But I gotta call them like I remember them.

It's a long time ago, but I can't remember any "I love you; you love me"—in the Reichert family of North Minneapolis—in the 1930s and 1940s.

My mother's siblings included two sisters and a pair of twin brothers—and a passion for long, loud, squabbling arguments—mixed with screaming and yelling—chaos, disagreement, misinterpretation, and misrepresentation. They would have made excellent politicians today.

We all lived close together in a middle-class, second-generation Jewish ghetto in North Minneapolis. We socialized together. We vacationed together. We celebrated holidays, anniversaries, birthdays, marriages, brises—together. And the three sisters fought each other—OVER EVERYTHING!

There was Aunt Dorothy, the eldest—a great cook—a world-class whiner—a nooj—a cheek pincher—but sweet and lovable (if she didn't drive you crazy).

Ida, our mother, was a little more hip. She thought Dorothy (Do) belonged in the middle ages—and made sure she was aware of it. Ida was a terrible cook—all grease and fat. She had a temper and mouth like a longshoreman—and tried to run the show.

Anne, the youngest, thought she was a beauty queen. She was quite attractive and attracted plenty of men. Her beauty was the centerpiece of her life and love. She was the last to get married—and felt put upon—whether she was or not.

The twin boys, Morrie and Hy, just tried to stay out of the line of fire—bobbing and weaving with the punches.

The sisters were known as "the Raging Reicherts." They fought each other over EVERYTHING. There was not a subject on which they agreed—homes, families, clothing, food, cars, jobs, children, religion—or what to fight about.

They went for the jugular in their intramural battles, but God had better be prepared if any outsider made any disparaging remark about any of the three. They immediately joined in mortal combat against the enemy—any enemy—and seldom were discouraged by rain, snow, sleet, or mud. Reicherts 3, The Enemy 0! And "Don't you ever say that about MY sister!"

Life as we knew it drastically changed one week every year—the week before Pesach. The entire mishpucha gathered in unity in Bubbe Reichert's kitchen—cooking—cleaning—loving—sharing—agreeing. No hassles. No disagreements. It was like an Israeli-Palestinian one-week peace treaty.

The antiseptically clean kitchen floor was covered with daily issues of the Jewish *Forward*—published in Yiddish.

The aroma of boiling chicken soup, matzah balls, homemade noodles, hard-boiled eggs, charosets, brisket, and kugel wafted to the rafters of Bubbe and Zayde's home. Round-faced little Bubbe took over sole management. Zayde, all the girls, their husbands, and the cousins paid homage at her tiny little feet—as she ran the operation like a gigantic soup kitchen. No arguing her commands. No question. You were told, and you did it.

The gigantic quantities of food were prepared daily—and disappeared into hot or cold storage areas—as directed. We marveled at what happened to the stacks of food that were prepared each day and disappeared each night.

It was a special week for the grandchildren. We were allowed to freely roam and examine the hidden treasures of Bubbe's closets and attics. A special attraction was the wind-up Victrola music machine—with scratchy records by Rudy Vallee, Al Jolsen, and Jimmy Durante. How we would love to have that old machine today.

We filled our faces with snack goodies that Bubbe would sneak to us during the day—while thinking about the magnificent meal awaiting us on Passover.

Erev Pesach culminated the week of PEACE, QUIET, LOVE—with the prayers from the Haggadah and the blessing over the cheap Passover wine. The length of the service depended on how many shots of schnapps Zayde downed before the service started. Each shot represented four or five skipped pages.

Did the RAGING REICHERT GIRLS EVER make it through the entire evening without a knock-down, drag-out? No way. Sometime—somewhere—some way—at some homes—there was peace and quiet and holiday spirit. But not at the Reicherts. There was always some unimportant matter that blew the lid off the chicken soup. What comes first, the chicken or the brisket? Who makes the kugel? Your matzah balls are too soft. Whose kids are making too much noise? I did more work than you!

By the time we stormed out of Bubbe's house, the only conversation was high-pitched yelling and screaming. We tried, but we never quite made a complete week. So don't tell me about your loving, joined-at-the-hips family. I know better. I've been there, done that. Passover peace—my chametz halla bread.

The Reicherts were early dysfunctional!

—*Bernie Meyers*

My family was Reform almost to the point of not having any religion. We did Erev Rosh Hashanah and Kol Nidre, but those were primarily social occasions. In addition, as my grandparents were born in the United States (somewhat of a rarity, I later came to learn) my family was extremely assimilated, as were most of the people with whom I grew up. I do not remember my parents ever having a Seder, nor did we attend one while my father was alive.

After my father died when I was twelve, some friends invited my mother and me to their house for Passover. These particular friends had the same religious (non) practices as we did, but my friend's uncle had married late and apparently found religion with his new young wife, so they put on what passed for a Seder in our circle. I recall that we mainly hit the high spots and then ate. A beautiful turkey, complete with stuffing was brought to the table. My mother was terribly impressed by the stuffing in particular and asked her friend's housekeeper how it was made. Liza replied, "Well, you take a loaf of bread. . . ." That was probably our last attempt at Passover.

—*Enid Blumenthal*

* * *

Happiness is having a large, loving, caring, close-knit family in another city.

—*George Burns*

* * *

My Passover memories are of the people who have stayed in my mind. I remember all my great-uncles talking in Hebrew and going on and on! And I fondly remember my great-aunts, who were so opinionated. Now my family says I'm the current generation of opinionated women!

—*Patty Nogg*

Passover, the occasion to usher in real freedom, can also be the inauguration of a newfound commitment to give people what they *really* need most.

A chance to speak.

An opportunity to be heard.

A comforting touch.

—Rabbi Yaacov Salomon

* * *

Parents can only give good advice or put them on the right paths, but the final forming of a person's character lies in their own hands.

—Anne Frank

They say insanity is hereditary: you get it from your kids.

—*Sam Levenson*

6

what's a girl like you doing at a seder like this?

A mini-manual for singles. After all, spending an evening in a room filled with relatives makes it hard to remain happily unattached!

Success in marriage does not come merely through finding the right mate, but through being the right mate.

—*Proverbs*

* * *

I ask you, my friend, who started all this business of marriage and wives?

—*Shalom Aleichem*

I'm a single, twenty-seven-year-old female, the oldest child and only daughter in a not-too-religious but fairly traditional Jewish family. Lately, as my grandparents get older and their health becomes fragile, I find that my whole family is putting increasing pressure on me to be dating seriously, moving toward marriage.

Well, on my brother's advice, I lied and told them I was seeing someone. Now, Passover is here, and they are expecting that I'll be bringing my "boyfriend!" But I'm hoping there is a kind, understanding soul who will answer this ad, who won't mind coming as my fake Passover date.

What I need you to be:

- Jewish—so you'll know the customs, etc. I'm not going to all this trouble only to have the family freaking out that I'm dating a non-Jewish boy!
- Age 28–35, or roughly thereabouts.
- Employed—they'll be asking you what you do.

- Outgoing and fun—my family is a big, goofy, fun-loving bunch.
- An intelligent conversationalist—my family loves to have friendly political debates. OK, I admit it: they're all lawyers—but nice ones!
- Handsome enough to make my grandma want to pinch your ass! (Don't worry, I'll protect you.)

What you'll get:

- The extreme gratitude of a kind, if duplicitous, female.
- A fantastic Passover meal.

Please be my fake Passover boyfriend.

—*Melissa Bernstein*

I have fond memories of the Passover Seders of my youth. Since we had no relatives in town, we always invited other newcomers who needed a place to attend Seder. As my sisters and I grew older, our father found families with sons or made sure that the male students from the nearby universities or young servicemen from the air force base were included.

—*Joyce Cohen*

* * *

Men who have pierced ears are
better prepared for marriage.
It means they've experienced
pain and bought jewelry.

—*Rita Rudner*

W hat do you do when six single women descend on your community Seder? Duck. And why is tonight different from all other nights? Because I'm sitting alone at Table 26, which the nice lady who took my credit-card number promised was designated for unattached men and women in their thirties and forties. All around me, men pull chairs out for their wives, young couples rock babies, and seventy-five-year-old women pull waiters aside to insist that their husbands cannot have salt with their meals. Here at Table 26, it's just me, all by my lonesome, at a table set for seven, and I'm staring at a bottle of grape juice, a bottle of Manischewitz, and a manipulate decked out with a slice of horseradish, a dollop of charoset, a thimbleful of salt water, and an abnormally small hard-boiled egg.

I spot a work friend of mine and wave to him, feigning bright-eyed goodwill. He and his Chinese girlfriend have chosen a young couples' table, and I'm tempted to switch seats. But just as I'm gathering up my things to join him, a fellow single named Susie takes a seat next to me. Just as we're exchanging pleasantries, two more women about our age settle in. One is a sturdy-looking dark blonde, and the other is a biochemist named June, who looks just like Ivana Trump in a black sequined top, that I'm sure she feels is wasted on present company.

We are soon joined by another attractive blonde who takes a seat to my left. We all begin to settle in, fast giving up hope that any men will join us. The rabbi calls for attention and explains that our table is our community and suggests we begin by introducing ourselves to the people who will be our "family" tonight.

Kiss the spirituality of the event good-bye. The table erupts into a cacophony of frustrations—women interrupting each other, women thumping the table for emphasis, and soon the rabbi and the kiddush chanting, along with the other 272 people in the dining room, have been forgotten.

Finally it's time for the actual meal, which the crowd ushers in with a rousing rendition of the story of the Four Sons, sung, oy gevalt, to the tune of *My Darling Clementine.*

We settle into eat, but not before Rebecca, a stunning redheaded latecomer, reports that there is a table of seven single men on the other side of the hall. It turns out we haven't been separated from the men as part of a religious protocol, but rather through an administrative glitch.

Forget all that milk and honey rigmarole. Table 11 is the new Promised Land. I take a deep breath and head over.

All I see before me is a circle of yarmulkes, and it's difficult to tell whether any of the men underneath them are attractive. "Please join us," I beg, pointing to our table. The men nod, smile, make enthusiastic motions to show that the minute they are through eating, they will report for duty, with pleasure. But an awkward silence follows, and that's when I blow it. I mention, nicely enough, that there has been some discussion at our table of the way all Jewish men seem to be controlled by their mothers. Glasses freeze in transit. Eyebrows rise. The warm welcome I originally received chills. None of the men stand up to follow us. I sulk back to the table in shame and inform the sisterhood that I have really goofed up.

Jennifer, Rebecca, June, Stephanie, and Susie all assure me that we don't need guys to have a good time. In other words, the good ladies lie.

Our conversation stops dead when a few intrepid bachelors do actually show up at our table. By now we are four ritual wine glasses into a celebration and so riled up over being single that the poor suckers don't have a chance. No Jewish matches have been made; although I leave with a backpack full of business cards from my seatmates. We go home drunk and full of macaroons.

—*Sheerly Avni*

* * *

Lift up your eyes and see what you
are choosing for yourself.
Do not set your eyes on good looks,
rather set your eyes on family.

—*Mishnah*

Passover Seders from 1943–45 were a communal experience shared by my mother, father, fifteen-year-old sister, and me, six to eight years old at an air force base in mid-Missouri with twenty Jewish air force guys!

My family was in a unique situation—one of a few Jewish families left in Sedalia, Missouri, a once thriving city with two hundred Jewish families, close to Whitman Air Force Base, thirty miles away. There were about twenty young Jewish men, most of them teenagers, stuck in a no-man's-Jewish-land for Pesach. My father was the lay rabbi of our small temple, designated rabbi by virtue of his ability to read Hebrew and Torah. How could we leave those men stranded and alone for the holidays? So my mom cooked, my dad prepared, my sister carefully selected her cutest outfit, and we packed up our matzah and other Passover goodies (which we schlepped from our shopping trip to Kansas City) and made our way to the base. I was thrilled to be the surrogate kid sister for many of these soldiers, and my sister fell madly in love with each and every one of them.

What Seders these were! It was an eclectic and motley crew from an orthodox officer from Brooklyn to a secular teen from Arkansas—all trying to make sense of this holiday and this life. They were all lonely, all grateful, and all very dependent on my family's empathy and hard work. I was so starstruck by those cute guys in their uniforms that I remember almost nothing of those Seders.

—*Willis Ann Ross*

* * *

I have often thought that every woman should marry, and no man.

—*Disraeli*

$\mathbf{O}$n a first date with someone new, we're thinking—why is this date different from all other dates? The courtship process has its own order, just like the Seder.

1. **Kadesh:** You set aside a time and place to meet. The first beverage arrives. The alcohol warms you, liberating you from the oppression of routine.

2. **Urhatz:** Before eating a morsel, someone excuses himself or herself to the washroom. This provides both partners a moment of solitude and a chance to assess the initial chemistry. If necessary ("I just got a call, something suddenly came up"), it's also an opportunity for an early, if not particularly graceful, exit.

3. **Karpas:** During hors d'oeuvres, you realize this is someone you wouldn't mind spending a few minutes with. You're not that hungry, but you could eat something.

4. **Yahatz:** You begin to share anecdotes about your lives. If you're lucky, this ends up a 50–50 give

and take, and no one can discern which half of
the conversation is bigger.

5. **Magid**: Now you're into the substance of your
date: the main narrative. As you tell your stories,
you find resonance in the experiences of someone
who moments before was a stranger at a strange
table. You have discovered which of the Four Sons
you are out with. (The wise son tentatively asks,
"What do you do? Do you like it? How'd you get
into that?" The wicked sons asks, "What redeem-
ing quality is there in that kind of career?" Because
he cannot see redemption in your choices, you
may smack him about the teeth, for he will not be
redeemed. The simple son asks, "Why are we
here?" and the fourth son, who doesn't even know
enough to ask, relies completely on you to pro-
vide the conversation, which you do politely before your exit.)

But tonight you're lucky; you're out with a wise son. You
bond over past professional servitude and shed the emotional

shackles of past relationships. You begin to feel as if you personally experienced your partner's suffering. You're so absorbed in your study of each other that you barely notice when the waiter approaches and says, "Rabotai, it's time to order dinner."

—*Esther Kustanowitz*

* * *

He who has no wife lives without joy, without blessing, and without good.

—*Talmud*

The Top Ten Passover Pickup Lines

10. Let's make this night really different from all other nights.
9. What will you do to me for two zuzim?
8. What's a girl like you doing at a Seder like this?
7. I'm going to have to search you for chametz.
6. Nice Haggadah.
5. Let's play "Hide the Afikomen."
4. I bet I could make you sing Dayenu!
3. Did that just say we were in bondage?
2. I could never *pass* you *over*. . . .
1. Hey pretty lady, why don't you and me make our own Exodus on over to my place?

You're a ten in my Haggadah.

—Anonymous

* * *

There is only one way to find out if a man is honest—ask him. If he says "yes," you know he's crooked.

—Groucho Marx

7

Next Year in Jerusalem or Australia or India

Every Seder ends with the hopeful phrase, "Next year in Jerusalem," but whoever thought of Australia, South Africa, India, Argentina, Russia, or Germany?

About thirty-five years ago, "when Russia was Russia," my wife Navah and I had the experience of celebrating Pesach in Leningrad (now called St. Petersburg). At the time, refuseniks were being severely oppressed by government authorities. For those who may not remember, refuseniks were Jews whose applications for visas to Israel had been refused. As a result, most of them had lost their jobs. Some of them had spent time in prison for trumped-up charges. All of them were deeply committed to being Jewish and were anxious to know more and more about our tradition, and most of them had been spending time studying Hebrew, Jewish sources, and books on Jewish religion and literature on varying levels.

We led Sedorim for a group of fifteen or twenty young people who never had been at a Seder before. We met in the apartment of a young married couple. That apartment had been chosen because one of its rooms did not share a wall with the adjacent apartment. So we could sing! It took a long time for everyone to gather, since more than two or three people coming together at the same time would have raised suspicions. We had brought Haggadot with Russian translations as well as a Seder plate and matzah cover. After everyone had introduced himself or herself, I led the Seder in Hebrew and in English. Those who knew neither language were helped by their friends who provided running Russian translations.

A tall young man wearing one of the yarmulkes we had brought recited the Four Questions in Hebrew slowly and correctly. As he did so, I felt a deep emotion similar to what I had felt when each of our own children recited those same words for the first time. Remember that almost all of them were hearing the words of the Haggadah for the very first time. Near the beginning of the narrative about our ancestors suffering as slaves in Egypt, a girl of about nineteen years old cried out: *zeh anachnu!* (This is us!); *heim yatz'u, anachnu neitzei* (They got out; we'll get out!). This set the tone of our conversations about the past, the present, and the future, all based upon the text of the Haggadah. As you might imagine, this Seder, including many questions, discussions, and songs, ended in the early hours of the morning.

After the Seder, we taught them Israeli songs, and Navah taught them Israeli dances that they were excited to learn. Just before the first people were about to leave the apartment, the girl who had shouted out *zeh anachnu,* holding the Seder plate, announced that as each of them left Russia, they would pass it on to other refuseniks, and that the last refusenik leaving would hand it to [Soviet Union president Mikhail] Gorbachev and turn out the lights.

—Rabbi Jules Harlow

* * *

In India, it is customary to pass the Seder plate over the heads of everyone at the table in a circular motion. It is an acknowledgment that, as the world turns, we were slaves first, then we became free.

—Leslie Koppelman Ross

I have lived through many Passovers, and my earliest memories are only now coming back. I see myself as a little girl in Poland, very excited about the coming Passover. At that time, my entire participation consisted of being given new dresses and new shoes. It was customary in our little town to outfit children from head to toe. So every year I went with my mother first to the dressmaker and then to the shoe store.

The comfortable, untroubled life I had known would come to an abrupt end when World War II began. I was eight years old. After being expelled from our town, I ended up in hiding, first alone, and then joined by my mother and sister.

The kind and brave woman who offered us shelter was illiterate; we did not have access to a newspaper or a calendar. We honestly did not know what month it was, or even what time of year it was. Today it is inconceivable, even to me, how primitively we lived.

One day my mother announced that the next day was the start of Passover. I have no idea how she invented that date. I was still at the age when I accepted my mother's statements at face value. So we celebrated Passover. At that time we had almost no money and lived entirely on bread and potatoes. For the next eight days we ate potatoes three times a day, never touching bread.

After the liberation, it took some time until we returned to a normal life. Some ten years later, my mother had passed away, and I was living in Western Europe. At an international book fair I met a Prince Charming—a young man with the bluest eyes in the world, tall and handsome, with impeccable manners. The man was of a different faith from my own, yet I was young and in love and did not think much about the consequences. On my birthday, he sent me beautiful roses. His calling card was imprinted with his family crest. He was of some European nobility. Even my father was impressed.

After some courting, the young man proposed. I was ready to accept. His mother wrote me a letter, inviting me to spend the Easter holiday with her in the family's villa in Nice, France, to get acquainted. I was young and very excited about the prospect. I accepted the invitation and started to pack for the holiday. Since I wanted to impress the mother, a very elegant lady, I asked my best friend, an Italian girl, Vittoria, to help me pack.

After filling the suitcase with my most precious outfits, I packed a box of matzahs. That year Easter and Passover fell at the same time. Vittoria, who was not Jewish, asked with surprise, "What is that for?"

"I never ate bread during Passover before and I do not intend to do so now," I answered.

Vittoria was appalled. "If you intend to spend your life with that fancy family eating matzah during Easter it will never work."

At that moment I remembered my late mother and her invented date of Passover. I realized that my roots were very strong, stronger even than my romantic desires. I did not go to Nice.

Very soon after, I left Europe for American, where I met a Jewish prince. A young man with the bluest eyes in the world, tall and handsome, with impeccable manners. We

celebrate Passover in our household, and to this day, I have
never eaten bread during the holiday.

—*Irene Frisch*

* * *

Passover is not a big holiday in Provence. The French
refer to Passover as *Pâques Jive,* Jewish Easter. Oy! My friend
Michael e-mailed from New York, "What's a French Seder
like?" I said, "Jewish, but with better wine." We were fourteen the first night—French, Belgian, English, Scottish, Aus-
tralian, Danish, American—but only two Jews counting
myself. Jews are not plentiful in this part of the world, just as
they aren't in the more rural areas of the United States. Two
houses down, the street where I live becomes the Rue Juiv-
erie which dates to the 1400s.

Finding Passover supplies in Provence is next to impos-
sible. My friend brought back Manischewitz egg matzahs
(seven dollars a box!) and matzah meal from the Rue des
Rosiers (Jewish quarter) in Paris. Every year I make brisket

the way my grandmother did for the Seder. There is no such cut in France. Meat here is done differently. That first year, Monsieur Dinelle and Monsieur Ghys, our local butchers, were anxious to help. The French cut of *paleron* seemed closest to what I needed. Dinelle supplied the chicken fat for my matzah balls and chopped liver; the meat and shank bone for the Seder plate I got from M. Ghys. Everyone was eager to help make my first Seder in Provence a success. Mme. Kittler, one of a handful of Jews living here, lent me her French-Jewish cookbooks. One, a tattered and worn paperback, was inscribed to her mother with the date Passover 1946. Mme. Kittler, whose first name is Daisy, was born in a concentration camp. Her mother had wanted to give her new baby a "typical" American name in honor of their liberators.

Finding fresh horseradish root for the Seder plate isn't possible—*raifort* is not in season, so I use grated horseradish cream found in the exotic foreign foods section of *Hypermarché LeClerc*, on the U.K. shelf, not far from Paul Newman's salad dressing and Old El Paso burrito mix on the U.S.

shelf. For my first Passover in Provence, I had decided I would make gefilte fish from scratch, as none is available here. After two separate attempts, suffice it to say even the two feral cats that came with my house turned their noses up and walked away. The morning of the Seder, into the *poubelle* (garbage) it went. The next year, my friend Tara air-mailed giant-sized jars of Manischewitz sweet gefilte as a gift in time for the Seder. It was an enormous success.

Last year I made my own Haggadahs on the computer, abbreviated, to be sure, as there are no Jews to savor and ponder the longer version. People still ask, do I miss New York, do I miss the States? My answer is always the same— no. I deeply love my new home. Provence for me is paradise. Ever since I started coming here, I confess now, when everyone else said "Next Year in Jerusalem!" at the end of the Seder, I quietly said to myself, "Next Year in Provence!"

—*Patricia Fieldsteel*

It was Pesach, some thirty years ago. We were celebrating the Seder with our family in Buenos Aries. My grandfather, Yankel, conducted it—reading the Haggadah, just as he did every year. My brother and I sang the songs. The Seder was unfolding in a joyful manner with its ritual steps, symbols, and songs.

At one point, my grandfather said to me in Yiddish, "Look well at how everything is done, because I am not going to live forever." I did not dare to reply. I only nodded my head. Some months later, my grandfather passed away.

I always remembered his words. They taught me that it is the responsibility of each younger generation to continue the tradition. I still hear the voice of my grandfather, and I now answer him with words I did not dare say at that time. "Don't worry. I looked well at how everything was done, and I shall do it. What you transmitted, I shall transmit."

—*Rabbi Mordechai Levin*

The first Passover Seder was held in occupied Germany on April 15, 1946.

I became the Jewish chaplain of the U.S. Third Infantry Division in November 1945. World War II had ended five months earlier. My job was to serve the division's Jewish personnel, and by agreement with my commanding general, I could also serve the Jewish survivors who lived in the division's area of occupation—an area that included the German cities of Kassel, Fulda, and Marburg.

Two months before the Seder, I was called in by Gen. Frank T. Schmidt to a general staff meeting. We were shown orders from ETO Headquarters (European Theater of Operations, headed by Dwight D. Eisenhower) alerting all commanders to the arrival of Passover and ordering them to enable Jewish personnel to celebrate the festival. This involved granting leaves, providing special foods, housing, and facilities to those desiring to observe Passover. I was told that my advice was needed in the implementation of those orders in the division. The number of Jews in the division was estimated to be about four hundred.

Someone in the general staff announced that a central location for the Seder would be in Kassel.

"But the city is completely demolished, bombed out," I said, questioning the choice of that city.

I was informed that there remained one underground bunker that was still operational. It was a huge area that could comfortably seat hundreds of people around banquet tables. When I began listing the special foods, wine, and Haggadot we would need, I was told that all those were already stipulated in an order from headquarters.

Before the staff meeting ended, I asked the general for permission to invite some of the Jewish survivors to take part in the Seder. The general, a sixty-something-year-old man, smiled and said, "If you invite me, you may invite them."

Within a week of that meeting, Passover staples began to arrive in two-and-a-half-ton trucks. The drivers fondly called the operation "The Matzah Ball Express." Matzah by the tons, wine by the gallons, gefilte fish by the truckload,

Haggadot by the case, nuts and apples by the bushels—even festival candles—began to arrive in my tiny office in Bad Wildungen, which I had to transship to Kassel.

Reports from regimental commanders indicated that about three hundred Jewish personnel signed up for the Seders in Kassel and that their transportation and housing were arranged. I then invited about one hundred survivors to join our Seder.

All day on April 15 trucks rolled in, bringing Jewish personnel from far-flung German cities. The Kassel bunker, with its special lighting and decorations, took on the look of a banquet hall of a first-class hotel.

Elegance was the order of the day. Even the dress code was not overlooked. The Seder was to be a full-dress affair—dark green jackets and pink pants for the officers and dress uniforms for the enlisted men. And the same for the survivors—"Shabbas clothes."

Before the Seder began, I asked our guests, the survivors, if they preferred to sit separately by themselves or to be interspersed with the military men. Since the biggest obstacle would be the language barrier, they opted to sit by themselves. I anticipated their reply, so I placed them near the head table, so they would feel welcome and, also, so that I would be able to talk to them in Yiddish throughout the Seder ceremonies.

Promptly at 7:00 p.m. the Seder began. The brass, led by the general, sat at the head table together with several survivors. Despite the huge turnout, we even managed to sneak in a brief evening service to set the tone for the night.

Things went well as we began with the Kiddush over the wine. Some joined in the traditional tune, but almost every one belted out the final prayer, "Blessed are you, O Lord . . . who kept us alive to reach this season." I then introduced the general, who addressed the gathering, welcoming both the military and civilian guests. His warm greetings were followed by one of the survivors, who led us in reciting, "This is the bread of affliction which our ancestors ate in the land of Egypt."

He had us in tears as he recounted the afflictions he and his fellow survivors suffered under the Nazis. Then he concluded expressing his happiness at being able to celebrate

their first Seder after five tortuous years. Finishing his re-
marks, he toasted the general, shook hands with him, then
turned to embrace me with tears in his eyes.

The response of the GIs and officers was spontaneous.
They walked over to the survivors' tables, toasting them—
embracing and kissing were the orders of the day. The delightful scene lasted for quite a while.

Now, I ask you, what could have gone wrong? Why did I
lose their attention when we got to the part of the Four
Questions? Why couldn't I get them to quiet down when we
tried to sing? Why didn't they listen to my repeated attempts
to describe the Four Sons or the ritual of maror and
charoset? Why did they continue toasting, talking, enjoying
each other rather than listening to me?

I will tell you the serious mistake I made—a detail that I
overlooked.

The waiters left all the wine bottles on the tables!

How could I forget this was the first time in years the
survivors had wine to drink? And how could I forget that, to
the soldiers, wine was the staff of life?

But there was a happy ending to this story. Either because of the wine or the many prayers, tables were switched. The military and the survivors began sitting with each other. Overcoming language and cultural barriers, they sang, they talked, and they enjoyed one another like long-lost relatives.

There was a flurry of papers being exchanged between the survivors and the military personnel. When I asked to see one of those pieces of paper, I realized the Americans were taking names of relatives in the United States whom they promised to contact on their return to the States.

And I can attest that they did observe the law: they did drink four—and maybe more—cups of wine as prescribed by our sages.

The surprise of the evening came when a group of survivors, joined by an equal number of U.S. soldiers, approached the head table and sang the Yiddish song, "Let us, all of us together, greet the general." After several repetitions, the group taught the song to the entire assemblage. They mingled with each other, totally eliminating the special seating arrangement we had originally made. They were definitely one family, celebrating a unique Passover Seder.

I will never forget what my commanding general said when he realized my distress at not being able to conduct a "proper" Seder. He put his arm around over my shoulder and his other over my chest.

"Son, don't worry," the general said. "You've never conducted a better Seder before, and you'll probably never conduct a better Seder in the future."

—*Rabbi Mayer Abramowitz*

* * *

My husband's Jerusalem employer transferred us to Sydney, Australia, where we arrived in late November—just in time for summer. I felt vaguely decadent about moving from one long stretch of summer beach on the Mediterranean to another one on the Pacific, as if I were fending off the real business of life while the rest of the world trudged off to school and work in the cold.

While the calendar read December, my internal preset winter clock wanted chicken soup. The world around me demurely sipped iced fruit shakes at outdoor café tables crowned with sun umbrellas.

Whatever temperature the thermometer recorded, the calendar still read Passover, and Passover would not be postponed due to weather, season, or location.

And so it is here, in Australia. I asked the rabbi in my Sydney community whether the Passover service is modified to accommodate the holiday's winter appearance. No, she replied, the service remains the same.

How remarkably comforting that was to me. Irrespective of place, our history and our calendar are constant. We are one voice chanting the story of our exodus from Egypt. Some of us may be on the threshold of spring while others are checking the insulation of our windows. But we are all standing together at the bank of the Red Sea, waiting for the waters to part, waiting to cross, anticipating our freedom.

—*Reb Carmel*

W alking through the land of Egypt, where our ancestors were once enslaved, seeing the ancient sites of Memphis, Sakara, and the Giza pyramids, and realizing that we would be making our own exodus back to Israel just in time for Pesach was remarkable. The joy of experiencing a physical return to our Jewish homeland was very spiritual. I could not wait to reenter the country in which I'd been living and studying for the past four months. I gained an even greater appreciation for Israel as a Jewish homeland than I already felt. To once again observe Passover in a land where I could speak the language, feel as comfortable to me as if being among family, celebrating with a nationwide community was an incredible feeling.

Every year in the Haggadah we read, "In every generation let each one feel as if he or she came forth out of Egypt." This year we were able to physically enact the statement as we returned to Israel from a five-day visit to Cairo two days before Pesach began.

—*Rebecca Murow*

There are about ten Jewish families in Delhi, all descendants of the B'nai Israel indigenous Indian Jews. Our Seder was held in an area of Delhi called Sunday Nagar, a wealthy subdivision where all the diplomats live. Our host was the political consultant for the Israeli Embassy.

There were about forty-five people at the Seder—Jews from all over the world—India, Israel, Italy, the United States, the United Kingdom, and one man from Bogotá, Columbia. The food was different, the melodies were different, but the feelings were the same. Everyone was just so happy to be there. There is something special about joining in a Seder in the middle of India.

—Rachel Jodie

* * *

For the Jews of southern Italy, the Jewish festival of Passover is a special celebration of beginnings. Like Jews the

world over, we gather at the traditional Seder table and remember how the Hebrew slaves, whom the angel of death
had miraculously "passed over," strapped sheets of unleavened bread to their backs. We recounted how our ancestors,
accompanied by righteous Egyptians who shared the Jewish
belief in slavery's inherent evil, stepped out on faith and
marched toward liberty. We ate the traditional foods, sang
the traditional songs, and toasted the birth of a new synagogue whose very existence gives testimony to the strength
and courage of the Jewish people.

Ner Tamid del Sud, the "Eternal Light of the South," represents the first organized rabbi-led synagogue to emerge in
the south of Italy (Calabria and Sicily) in what some historians say is more than five hundred years. Gathering at the
Passover table in Palermo (Sicily) and Platania (Calabria),
Italians whose Jewish roots and traditions were all but de-
stroyed by local persecutions—including the Spanish Inqui-
sition—dipped "sedono" (celery) into vinegar and
remembered the bitterness of those days when Jews were

driven from their homes in the larger cities of Calabria and Sicily and forced to flee into the mountains.

"Platania is a good place for the Seder," said one of our guests who just discovered his grandmother's Jewish roots. "Just being here reminds me of how far we had to go to try to keep our traditions alive." From our Seder table we could see the high mountains of Calabria that in mid-April were just beginning to turn green. Nearby were the small villages of Tiriolo, Decolatura, Serrastretta and Zangarona, each one with a "Via di Judeca," small enclaves that form the remnant of Calabria's strong and vibrant Jewish past, which is just now beginning to be documented.

Angela Amato is a concert violinist living in Milan who, along with her six-year-old son, Alessandro, attended our Seder in Sicily. Angela is part of a dedicated group of Jewish families who work hard to bring Jewish tradition back to southern Italy and who believe that celebrating major Jewish festivals is one way to make that happen. And it seems to be working. For our Passover Seders, law student Marco Marcellino learned all the Seder blessings, Viviana prepared the ceremony for kindling the holiday candles, and ceramic artist Salvo Parrucco assisted as Seder leader. It is Salvo's dream not only to revive Jewish tradition in his native Sicily but to become a rabbi as well.

As our Seder meals ended, in Sicily with Angela Amato's violin solo, "Yerushaliayim Shel Zahav" (Next year in Jerusalem) and in Calabria with a rousing "Avinu Shalom Alechim" (Hello, Friends), the sixty-plus participants kissed on both cheeks, Italian-style, hugged each other, and wished a hearty "Chag Sameach" (which is Hebrew for "Buona Festa") and "Happy Holiday." In the strength of our embrace we felt the strength of Jewish traditions that represent an important Passover sentiment. For us, the Jews of southern Italy, hope never dies.

—Rabbi Barbara Aiello

* * *

I served for three years as rabbi of Temple Israel Greenpoint in Cape Town, South Africa. I arrived just a few months after apartheid ended, and the Jewish community was still very worried about what would happen. The first Passover was very emotional, because Passover, of course, is the holiday of freedom, and South Africans were celebrating their freedom from oppression that entire year.

We held a Seder in our community hall the first night of Passover. There were about sixty people, a relatively small crowd for such a large congregation. Nevertheless, the diversity was enormous. One of our congregants was a Zulu who had adopted Judaism many years earlier. He was a medical doctor by training and was serving in a high position in the new government. There were also a number of people there who had been active in the anti-apartheid struggle.

We also had some tourists, including a delightful French family. There were American Jews as well, most of whom were active Reform Jews. They were a bit surprised to see how similar things were. There are about fifteen other synagogues, but they were all Orthodox. They were generally quite hostile to us, seeing Reform Jews as apostates and Reform Judaism as heresy. It was very unpleasant, and I tried to become friendly with the various Orthodox rabbis in an attempt to break down those barriers. They were civil to me, but it didn't really help our institutional relationships.

While I saw Passover as an expression of the freedom that the country was experiencing, my impression was that most South African Jews saw Judaism as something that spoke about the past and not the present. Most yearned for the good days that they felt were gone forever. The chief rabbi, who has recently passed away at a very young age, tried his best to encourage South African Jews to participate in the creation of a new democratic society. Relatively few were interested. Many were planning to emigrate to Australia and, when Australia became difficult, to New Zealand. For some, that Passover was to be their last in South Africa, a country where their families had lived for about a hundred years.

—*Rabbi Dana Evan Kaplan*

8

Let My people Enjoy

Humor in Judaism dates back to the Torah.
According to tradition, we are commanded to
sing, study, and enjoy the Jewish holidays.

Once a year most of us in the entertainment field take a day off to watch or attend the Academy Awards. In my house, it's called passover.

—*Bob Hope*

While few of the traditional Seder foods trace their origins as far back as matzah, it should be noted that the lowly horseradish root also crossed the Red Sea with the fleeing Israelites.

As impoverished slaves, they had access to few vegetables, and the hard and woody horseradish was a household staple.

While most of the fleeing Israelites carried with them horseradish, there is a story told of one family where, while gathering up their few belongings, discovered that they had no horseradish left in their house. The wife sent her husband into the field to dig up a large horseradish root, but in the darkness and confusion, he unearthed a large ginger root by mistake.

The story continues that after forty years of wandering in the desert, the Israelites finally entered the promised land. But it was another year before the family with the ginger arrived to settle among the rest of the Israelites.

When asked where they had been, the matriarch of the family, now grown old, shrugged and answered, "My husband insisted on taking an alternate root."

—*Anonymous*

* * *

A man took his Pesach lunch to eat outside in the park. He sat down on a bench and began eating. A little while later a blind man came by and sat down next to him. Feeling neighborly, he passed a sheet of matzah to the blind man. The blind man ran his fingers over the matzah for a few minutes, looked puzzled, and finally exclaimed, "Who wrote this nonsense?"

—*Anonymous*

Every year we had this great group of forty or fifty relatives for passover, and my brothers and I would entertain them and make them laugh.

—*Billy Crystal*

I can still hear my mother saying, "Could you send me the name of a caterer that could do the whole dinner?"

—*Gail Kohll*

* * *

I wish Passover wouldn't pass over so quickly!

—*Joey Bishop*

Top Ten Similarities Between the NCAA Tournament and Passover

10. March Madness is what you call the month prior to Pesach when you clean your house.

9. The Final Four is a clear reference to the Four Sons.

8. Dick Vitale shares the same hairstyle as Yul Brynner.

7. Sweet Sixteen is the unmentioned final step of the Seder night: Going to sleep drunk.

6. Wildcats, Longhorns, Terrapins, Hawks, and Tigers add up to one crazy dose of Arbah.

5. Talk about snubbed the Jews were put in the lowest bracket for over two hundred years.

4. After all is said and done, the Egyptians are definitely going to be upset.

3. You call your number-one pick "The Chosen People."

2. At the Big Dance (Sinai), the Jews became the sleeper.

1. NCAA is actually one of the last acronyms of Rabbi Gamliel: Negotiate Cash for Afikomen Abduction.

—Isaac and Seth Galena

If Jews were more honest about their holidays, I think Passover would be called, "The Joyous Week of Constipation"—Bad Food, Lousy Food, and Constipation. There is a reason why we make a point of eating prunes and other dried fruits this holiday.

—*Judi Sohn*

* * *

Jews work so hard all year. passover comes around, and there's not a piece of bread in the house.

—*Milton Berle*

A leading Israeli rabbi has ruled that the anti-impotency pill Viagra can be taken by Jews on Passover, reversing a previous ban. Viagra had been deemed not kosher since 1998 under strict dietary laws. Anticipating the week-long Jewish spring holiday, Rabbi Mordechai Eliahu said the pill could be swallowed if it is first encased in a special soluble kosher capsule. Viagra's Israeli manufacturers said they had sought relief after receiving queries from worried religious men who wanted to obey Judaism's dietary laws and still be the most popular guy at the Bar Mitzvah. Word of the rabbi's ruling was greeted with glee and dancing.

—*Robert Darden*

Top Ten Signs Your Seder Is Too Big

1. When Elijah shows up, you give him his wine "to go."
2. When you read the list of the Ten Plagues, the word "locusts" really ring.
3. Even the kids complain that they do not have enough maror.
4. While waiting for everyone to wash their hands the second time, the matzah goes stale.
5. You start looking at ads for closed circuit TVs and auxiliary speakers.
6. When you rotate verses of "Echad Mi Yodea?" someone ends up singing, "Who Knows 39? I Know 39."
7. You have to use a microscope to divvy up the knaidlach.
8. You have to sketch your living room/dining room on graph paper first.
9. To recline at the table, everyone has to do it in unison.
10. You can't find anywhere out of sight to hide the Afikomen.

—Anonymous

I once wanted to become an atheist, but I gave it up because they have no holidays.

—*Henny Youngman*

* * *

They tried to kill us. We won. Let's eat.

—*Anonymous*

glossary

afikomen: hidden piece of matzah

Bubbe: Grandmother

Chad Gadya: Passover song sung at conclusion of Seder

chametz: leavened grain products that are not acceptable for Passover

charoset: mixture of apples, nuts, and wine

Dayenu: Passover song that means "it would have been enough"

Elijah: the prophet for whom we symbolically open the door

erev: night before a holiday

gefilte fish: mixture of chopped fish

Haggadah: book used at the Seder, means telling

Haggadot: plural for Haggadah

Halacha: Jewish law

halla: special bread for Shabbat and festivals

Hallel: seasonal blessing

hillel sandwich: sandwich made with a mixture of matzah, bitter herbs, and charoset

hazzan: other word for Cantor

karpas: parsley on the Seder plate

kibbutz: chat

glossary

Kiddush: blessing over wine

knaidlach: another word for matzah balls

Kol Nidre: prayer chanted on Yom Kippur Eve

kugel: noodle or potato baked dish

Ma Nishtanah: four questions asked at the Seder

maror: bitter herbs used at the Seder

matzah: unleavened bread eaten during Passover

matzah brie: fried matzah with eggs

matzah balls: balls made of matzah meal and eggs and served in chicken
soup

matzah meal latkes: fried pancakes

mazon: charity to help people who are hungry

midrash: stories from biblical sources

mishpucha: family

oy gevalt: Yiddish for "Oh No!" "No way!"

Passover: spring festival commemorating the Pesach (Passover)

Pirkeh Avot: collection of Rabbinical sayings and proverbs

rabatai: untraceable word meaning "Oh ye assembled"

refuseuiks: Russian Jews unable to leave Russia

Rosh Hashanah: Jewish New Year

schmoozing: chatting

glossary

Seder: Passover service, literally order
Sedorim: plural for Seder
shabbat: Sabbath, day of rest
shalom: hello or peace or good-bye
shlepped: carried
shtetl: village
Talmud: Torah commentaries
Torah: first five books of the Hebrew Bible
tovu vavohu: disorder, chaos
tsimmes: a mixture of carrots, prunes, and meat
unleavened: foods without flour
yarmulke: head covering
yeshiva: Jewish school for Torah study
Yom Kippur: Day of Atonement
Yom Tov: high holidays

acknowledgments

I offer my sincere appreciation to the many contributors to this book. This Passover project would not have been possible without their wonderful, original Seder memories. Special thanks go to Rabbi Barbara Aiello, spiritual leader of Synagogue Ner Tamid del Sud in Calabria in the "toe" of Italy's boot; Isaac and Seth Galena from www.bangitut.com; Beth Panetz, National Restaurant Association; Rabbi Jeffrey Rappoport, Kosher Nexus; and Lee Ratzan of Jewish Magazine (www.jewishmag.com).

To Andrea Gross, your wise advice and never-ending encouragement always inspired me. And to Ron Pitkin, who said, "I like the idea of your book!" I am truly grateful.

But most of all, I am thankful to have the two finest daughters anyone could ever wish for: Amy Levine and Wendy Katzman.